Why Didn't I Hear About This Earlier?

INVESTORS OFTEN DON'T KNOW
WHAT THEY'RE MISSING

Mark Roberts
with Rick Dean

Affinity Asset Management
OVERLAND PARK, KANSAS

Mark Roberts/Affinity Asset Management
13220 Metcalf Ave., Suite 220
Overland Park, KS 66213
www.affinityasset.com

Book layout ©2013 BookDesignTemplates.com

Ordering Information:
Quantity sales. Special discounts are available on quantity purchases by corporations, associations, and others. For details, contact the "Special Sales Department" at the address above.

Why Didn't I Hear About This Earlier?/ Mark Roberts. —1st ed.
ISBN 978-1537303437

Contents

What you don't know *can* hurt you 5

    Teaching the teacher 8

    You don't know what you don't know 11

The escape of the captive company man 13

    The good hands man 14

    Taming the tax beast 16

    The four corners of Affinity 18

Working with a full toolbox 21

    The independent vs. the "captive" advisor 21

    Understand how your advisor is compensated 24

Know the rules of a game we all must play 27

    The three buckets 28

    Pros and cons 31

    Maximize your 401(k) 35

Pay me now or pay me later 37

    The numbers game 38

    No good deed goes unpunished 40

Stretch out your retirement savings.................................43

    The $5,000 example...44

    Don't wait until age 70 ½.......................................46

    Don't ignore the tax strategies................................52

    Think of your heirs...55

It's not enough to win on paper.................................57

    The difference Bill could have made 59

    I ask again: Why haven't I heard this before?...........66

Who's looking out for your money? 69

    Money management models....................................70

    Hope for the best, prepare for the worst 73

    Be ready for the rally...78

Never stop learning 83

    Knowledge helps develop trust...............................85

    The University of Roth 86

    Turning investments into income...........................88

The culture of Affinity 91

CHAPTER 1

What you don't know *can* hurt you

Here at Affinity Asset Management, we feel fortunate to advise people who've done a lot of things right when it comes to their financial affairs. People who've worked hard, saved, invested and planned ahead well enough to have reasonable expectations of a comfortable life in retirement.

They are the kind of people a financial services advisor feels blessed to have as clients.

But even clients with solid work and saving habits — and perhaps an advanced understanding of financial matters — often need help in navigating the road to retirement. They find themselves not completely on track to getting where they ultimately want to be, mainly because they're playing a game in which they don't know all the rules. They're not playing it wrong, mind you, but they're also not taking advantage of everything they could since they don't know all the game's strategies.

That's why I'm not surprised when, after advising new clients — among them a community college business teacher and an estate attorney — about income tax strategies that might save them thousands of dollars in retirement, a comment I hear frequently is "I wish I'd heard about this earlier."

This comment often comes from people I just met who tell me they really like their current advisor, but that they had learned something new from me in an introductory 30-minute meeting. In introducing myself and sharing how we are similar and how we are different from other financial advisors, a new client might learn something they didn't know despite years of meetings and conversations with their current advisor.

Helping clients maximize their hard-earned retirement savings through income tax strategies and money management is something we take great pride in at Affinity, our full-service financial services firm in the Kansas City suburb of Overland Park, Kansas.

In the upcoming chapters of this book, we will explore strategies and management techniques we used to help estate attorney Ron Wilson — an invented name for a real person, as will be the case with the names of all clients identified in this book — make the retirement commitment he didn't think he was ready to make. Or the way we helped Flynn Robinson, a personal finance teacher who had been hit hard by the 2008 recession, reduce the risk that made his impending retirement seem less likely. Or the confidence we helped bring to the Christophers, a retired couple who were reluctant to try something new at an advanced age.

All of these folks had their own investments and their own financial advisors, people they trusted long before I met them. They'd been given good advice, made generally good decisions, did most of the right things in the earning phase of their working lives.

And yet I still managed to surprise them, opening their eyes to options and strategies they didn't know about that increased their prospects for stability in the often uncertain world of retirement.

This is a theme you will see throughout this book. In our opinion, clients should expect more from their financial advisors than what they are getting, and many don't even realize what they are missing. Because this business is built on relationships, we find new clients all the time who have loved and trusted their previous advisor. Yet, after meeting with us, they realize there are planning strategies they could have implemented long ago that may have made a significant impact on their money.

The title "financial advisor" is often used incorrectly, in my opinion.

The average person thinks a financial advisor is someone who will advise on all aspects of the financial world. People assume if something is important for them to know, their financial advisor will tell them about it.

In reality, most financial advisors are really investment or product advisors. They will sell you a good product and even advise on diversification. But too many people don't know what questions to ask of such advisors. Consequently, they assume their advisor will inform them of anything they need to know that will improve their financial outlook.

We hear time and time again from new clients that, not only did their advisor not discuss retirement or income planning, they also didn't discuss some of the basics of the products they were selling, aspects such as the level of risk involved or the fee structure. When we at Affinity Asset Management share information on fees and risks with new clients, some are surprised that this hadn't been shared with them previously.

That's why it's important for advisors to remember that clients have their own professions and are not financial experts. We have to assume that they often don't know the right questions to ask, and that we have to open their minds and help teach them.

Teaching the teacher

Consider the case of Flynn Robinson, the finance instructor I just mentioned. A very bright guy, he knew how to teach the workings of stocks, bonds, mutual funds and personal finance. He also felt he knew almost everything there was to know about saving for retirement.

He was maybe five years from retirement when we first met, and already was on a good track to that goal. He had a defined state pension and Social Security — a decent amount of fixed income. He and his wife had saved and invested regularly through a 403(b) plan at work and other investment vehicles scattered all over the place.

He didn't realize it, but he was already in what I call "retirement mode," with the reasonable expectation that he could leave the workaday world at any time of his choosing and live off the assets he had gathered in his working years.

But even with all of that, Flynn didn't really have a retirement plan. He did have his own spreadsheets that projected his assets to see if he would run out of money or not. Those spreadsheets, however, didn't take into account everything he needed to feel totally comfortable pulling the trigger on retirement. He was like a lot of people who have goals and save toward reaching those goals, but don't have a blueprint in place that lets them see if they're on track to reach them.

Flynn thought he had done his homework. He did the basic math, estimated he would need X amount each month to live on in retirement, then deducted his incoming pension and Social Security income from that outgoing amount. The remainder was a gap he figured he could cover from savings and investments.

What he didn't account for, however, were things like the different rates of return on savings and investments, inflation and, most significantly, the different kinds of income taxes he would be facing. Those often-overlooked elements can cast a shadow on anyone's otherwise optimistic retirement picture.

It wasn't until we sat down with Flynn and his wife and put all their investments together and talked about their goals that we were able to put together a comprehensive financial plan.

We did the things we do best, starting with a good factfinder of all their accounts and their goals and wishes. We first consolidated and repositioned some investments that reduced a lot of the risk and volatility that really hurt him during the 2008 recession, when he lost in a year and a half what it took him four years to get back. We then identified ways to create income streams and save on taxes to help make sure he didn't run out of money.

When Flynn looked at the things we were suggesting, he soon saw he could save a considerable amount on income taxes over the rest of his life. Saving on income taxes means having more of your money available to grow, or more of your money to spend. Either way, saving on income taxes is a win-win.

Like most people, he had much of his savings and investments in what I call the tax-deferred or tax-delayed "left bucket" of the three-bucket savings model we'll use throughout this book. It is the dominant bucket of the three. Most people have a smaller amount in the taxable, or middle bucket, but almost nothing in the tax-*favorable* right bucket of Roth IRAs and municipal bonds that can provide considerable tax savings in retirement. [1]

Later on, we will illustrate the tax savings gained over the long haul from making a steady, systematic transfer of assets — starting even before retirement age, and certainly before the government's required minimum distributions (RMDs) kick in at age 70 ½ — from the tax-deferred (left) bucket to the tax-*favorable* (right) one.

---

[1] All references to tax buckets and the rules governing them are based on tax law in effect at the writing of this book in 2015.

The philosophy behind this approach is simply stated. When you save money on taxes, you have more money to spend or more money to grow. And for most people whose biggest concern in retirement is making sure they don't run out of money, a financial plan that provides for spending less in taxes can make a huge difference.

For Flynn and his wife, this transition of their tax burden from tax-deferred to tax-*favorable* status is a work in progress. This is by design. Start the tax strategies now and keep doing these small things every year for the rest of your life.

We never try to balance the buckets drastically, as transferring assets out of the tax-deferred bucket always incurs a tax liability, and you don't want that to be too great in any single year. But remember, Uncle Sam will eventually claim his cut of your money that has been growing tax deferred/delayed for years in 401(k) accounts, IRAs, annuities, pensions and your Social Security pool. Paying some of that tax during your earning years, when you are likely to have deductions to offset the hit, is preferable to paying taxes in retirement when deductions are hard to find.

To be clear, the Robinsons were like most of the clients we meet, well on their way to retirement or already retired. Even without our help, their income and assets are usually in solid shape. In most cases, they are never going to run out of money.

Still, through the planning strategies we designed, we saved them taxes and helped lower the risk of depleting their retirement savings. By doing this, their money had an even bigger cushion. There was more for them to spend, or more to pass down to their family. Doing these strategies typically doesn't cost anything; it simply involves knowing the rules to your money and having strategies that are more than mere projections. Their cake was already baked through their own hard work and planning. We came in with the extra icing that made retirement potentially sweeter.

You don't know what you don't know

Helping people with tax strategies that can stretch their retirement savings is just one of the things we do at Affinity, but it's something we think sets us apart from other advisors. All doctors don't have equal abilities. All attorneys don't have equal abilities. All tax preparers don't have equal abilities, so please understand that all financial advisors do not have equal abilities. Too many people assume they do.

Giving clients options they had not gotten previously from other advisors, then seeing the positive results after they execute those options, is one of the joyful aspects of my job. Helping clients reach their life goals in savings is so very rewarding, and an awesome responsibility.

Take the case of Ron Wilson. A very intelligent, very confident estate planning attorney, he had three financial advisors prior to meeting us. He and his wife had done a phenomenal job of saving money along the way, but he still had kids in college and had turned over a lot of assets in a divorce. Despite building a nice nest egg, he still didn't know if he could pull the trigger on retiring in his early 60s.

We sat down with him, did a full analysis and developed a plan using tax and income strategies that gave him confidence that he was ready to take that step. One year after we met him, he was ready to go into retirement and play a lot of golf.

The Christophers, John and Sheryl, were already retired when we first met them. They were in their 70s and had done a great job of saving in a lot of investment vehicles with several different companies — 32 different accounts we had to address, most of them in tax-deferred or taxable buckets.

They were like many others with good investments, but they were spread out in too many accounts. We were able to consolidate many of those investments into fewer accounts without having to sell out of those investments. They kept their good investments, but by moving those into fewer accounts, the Christophers were able to watch and monitor their investments more easily. Although there may be some small costs involved with closing accounts, consolidating investments into fewer accounts doesn't cost anything with Affinity Asset Management.

They were excited that we weren't out to move them out of all their investments and sell them all new ones. They loved the idea of consolidation because, as they get older, they found it harder to follow and track what their money was doing.

At first I wasn't sure how much I could help them. A lot of folks I meet in their 70s, quite frankly, are reluctant to make big changes. It doesn't matter what the change is or how it may benefit them — they're stuck in their ways, to a degree.

But the Christophers weren't like that. They listened as we explained some income strategies they hadn't heard from anybody else, and it didn't take long before they bought into our process.

They became like so many of our clients who learn how to save a tremendous amount in taxes by doing some very fundamental things they haven't done before. They're now in a place where all the financial concerns they hear people talk about on television become just background noise.

These folks are delightful to work with. After all, they did all the hard work. They had to save it before I could help protect and grow it. Now they're living the good life — in part because of the help we gave them.

That's what this book is about. It's about having the blueprint, the money management techniques, the tax strategies and the right people on your side to help give you a low- or no-stress retirement.

CHAPTER 2

The escape of the captive company man

L ooking back on my days with a big company, they should have been some of the happiest times of my life.

I was selling investment products by age 22, and I was very, very good at it. I was one of the company's top producers every year. For 12 years, I always made the vacation trips the company awarded to its top salesmen, and was even featured in the firm's employee recruitment videos. I was on pace to be the youngest person inducted into the company Hall of Fame.

Yet somehow it didn't feel right. I felt limited by the products the company asked me to use. I knew the advisor was more important than the products; basically, a great advisor with so-so products is better than great products sold by a so-so advisor. In my opinion, clients should not judge an advisor by what he sells them, but rather by what he does after he has your money, since it is the long-term work that makes the biggest difference.

I wanted to do more to better serve my clients. I grew tired of being limited, tired of being told what products to sell. Sure, the investment products I sold were an improvement on what my clients owned previously, but they also were not as good as what I could offer as a completely independent advisor with access to many varieties of options.

So, in January of 2008, at the ripe old age of 33, I started out on my own without a parent company's support, and also without the handcuffs.

Even before that, I understood that establishing relationships and building trust means everything to a financial advisor. That's why I'm taking just a few pages here to briefly tell you about me — how I got here, how I came to develop the strategies I employ today, and why I believe that what I've learned along the way can make a difference in your retirement.

In that time, I've learned more about myself and what it means to be a professional as opposed to merely being a friend.

Don't get me wrong — I love my relationships with my clients, and many of them have turned into good friends along the way. However, we get a lot of referrals, and I want that referral to come to us because of the organization we have and what we do as opposed to "Mark is a really nice guy."

At the end of the day, clients would rather entrust their money to someone they know will get the job done as opposed to giving it to a person they like as a friend. This is probably why I don't ask to do business with friends. When someone is a friend first, I don't even like to talk money. I'll help them in any way I can and answer their questions, but I will not pursue them as clients. My clients that are friends now were clients first. That is, our client-advisor relationship was established long before the friendship developed.

The good hands man

I started out selling car and home insurance right out of high school, and continued through college, when I took 12 hours a semester and made up the difference in summer school. I worked for a well-known Missouri agency that sold the products of a major brand-name company. I quickly learned the importance of explaining something that was not in the vocabulary of most people — insurance — in a way they could understand. I was good at this, and I was making the agent I worked for a lot of money. I was organized and structured everything; most importantly I structured and managed my time.

When I was 22, that major insurance company approached me, asking if I was interested in becoming an agent and working for myself. I was super flattered. They were offering me my own office, orphan clients, a base salary to start with, and all the equipment and technology I needed. It sounded awesome.

But I also knew that selling insurance would never be my passion. With my college degree in business and an emphasis on finance, I wanted to sell investments and help people better handle their money. But I also very much liked the idea of being my own boss.

So, at the age of 22, I accepted another offer to become a financial advisor, to run my own office selling investments with the support of a major parent company. This was much better. I got additional training, a salary to start, a few (but very few) orphan clients and investment products to sell. I was on the path to where I wanted to go.

It was a sink-or-swim situation. Though the insurance company was willing to give me a lot of prospective clients, my new financial parent offered up only a few with whom to start. Obviously, they wanted to see what this 22-year-old kid could do. I had to learn how to find prospective clients fast, learn to talk to strangers about money, learn how to get referrals by setting myself apart from other financial advisors.

This company-managed sales force sold a variety of company-owned investment products to a clientele that was limited to nationwide members of a particular religion. That's right; its advisors were allowed to work only with clients of a certain faith, one whose churches were helped by the financial company's profits. Not only was I limited in the products I could sell, but I was super limited in the clientele. But at least I was finally selling investment vehicles such as mutual funds and variable insurance — something other than the car and home casualty policies I had been selling.

I felt I was taking the next step up. Better yet, I was very successful.

But even then there was something missing. I was a 20-something, commission-based salesman trying to sell investment products to people two, three times my age. Why, they wondered, should they entrust their hard-earned money — the money being saved for their future — to someone so young and green?

That's when I knew that to set myself apart, to grow and be something different, I had to offer something few other financial advisors spent much time discussing. Something that was a common problem for everyone, but wasn't being addressed by the people I saw working around me.

Something such as strategies to help reduce taxes.

Taming the tax beast

Back in those days, estate taxes were a popular topic, as the limits an estate could pass to heirs were much lower than they are today. So, I looked for opportunities to get my clients to an estate planning attorney who could handle their wills, trusts and powers of attorney, and who could help them build their own estate plans.

I sat in on every meeting, learning and soaking up everything the attorney said. By doing this, I was helping protect my clients' estates from final expenses such as probate, inheritance taxes and estate taxes.

I did this from about age 22 to 25 before I started getting restless with this kind of planning. It really wasn't helping me much in selling financial products or solving other issues, because everything I did was centered on what happened when people died. I thought it was more interesting to talk about their interests when they were alive.

That's when I began to study income taxes backward and forward, and even dabbled briefly with the idea of becoming a certified public accountant (CPA). I didn't go that route after deciding I couldn't be an expert in both the financial services and tax industries. There are those who handle both financial advice and accounting, but I didn't want to be in a position where I wasn't paying enough attention to my clients' investments during the busy tax season from January through April. I also didn't want the continuing education requirements of two very large industries. In my opinion, any professional that crosses into two industries is not a specialist, they are a generalist — e.g., an attorney who also does income tax returns, or an accountant who also sells investments.

Still, my exposure to the estate planning attorney greatly expanded my knowledge of tax matters and helped me find my niche. That is, to become an advisor who would emphasize minimizing one's tax income burden as a key component in managing investments and planning for retirement. After all, not everyone has estate tax, inheritance or probate problems, but we all hope to pay less income tax. Given that common ground, why not talk more about that with clients?

So, I changed my path to something more interesting to me, and something that affects all my clients at any level of income or asset size. Still young at 25, I set out to be that advisor who was great at money management and building retirement plans, and who specialized in the long-term reduction of income taxes. Again, less money spent on income taxes means more money available to spend or grow.

There was one more step to take, and in 2008 I took it. In establishing my own company, Affinity Asset Management, I was now free of the constraints of a parent company. As a completely independent advisor, I felt I finally had a complete toolbox at my disposal. To be sure, I'd had success as a captive advisor selling only the products of a parent company. But so often that felt like pounding a round peg into a square hole. I much prefer being the independent advisor who can look objectively at a wide range of investment options that may fit the specific needs of a client.

My business model didn't really change after leaving the parent company and going completely independent. I ran my appointments and operations the same, and had the same staff working for me. I changed the company name and logo, which I felt was important for my clients and the team around me. Much of our success is due to the brilliant people I have surrounded myself with at Affinity Asset Management.

The four corners of Affinity

A brief word here about the Affinity name and company logo.

I was looking for a name that showed there was more to my company than "Mark Roberts Financial." I did not want to be seen as a one-person operation, but as a growing company in which the mission was so much more important than any individual. My wife, Amy, and I set out to find a name that was more encompassing and yet had significant meaning for me. We initially tried all kinds of words and combinations without liking anything.

Then one night over dinner, Amy said, "I think I know the answer, but let me ask anyway. What is the most important part of your job as it relates to your clients?" I replied, "That's easy, it's my relationships." Even though we were in the middle of dinner, she got up, went to the computer, consulted a Thesaurus, looked up a synonym for "relationship" and found "affinity." Thus, the Affinity Asset Management name was born.

The logo — four puzzle pieces in bright, prime colors — came even easier. It reflects the four pieces of a retirement plan that must fit together to make a comprehensive plan:

- Money management, making the most of the investments in the plan.
- Tax strategies, moving assets around in the three tax buckets.
- Distribution design, creating income streams to be used in retirement.
- Developing the actual plan that puts everything together.

Too many financial advisors don't do all that. They sell a product, even a good product, or perhaps they even project a retirement plan without considering all the implications of Social Security, tax strategies, RMD rules or the value of holdings in different tax buckets. But there is so much more that has to be done, meaning you may have to do more than you are doing now to enjoy real financial security and confidence in retirement. The earlier in life you start, the more tax savings you will see.

A talk I had with a prospective new client illustrates the point.

He was telling me that his current advisor of many years had done a great job. I won't identify the advisor's company, but let's give it the mythical name, "Tax Savings Group." As we continued talking, I was stunned to learn that his advisor had never suggested any tax strategies, not even anything as simple as an IRA to Roth IRA conversion. I had to ask, just to verify, "Your advisor's company name is Tax Savings Group, yet in all your time with them they never advised on any tax-saving strategies?"

"How ironic," the gentleman said with a chuckle.

CHAPTER 3

Working with a full toolbox

There is a basic question any investor needs to ask early in a relationship with a financial advisor. That is:

"Is this advisor working for me, or is he working for his company?"

The difference — which too few people truly understand — can impact your ability to build a solid retirement plan. The difference is the reason I wanted to run my own independent advisory firm, one where I could respond to the specific needs of my clients rather than the sales directives of the home office.

The difference is significant enough that I thought it necessary to spend a few pages discussing it.

The independent vs. the "captive" advisor

Most financial advisors fit into one of three categories.

One is what I call the "captive advisor" who can sell only the investment products of the company for which he works. He sells most of the same kind of investments as any other agent, and many are good investment products. Still, a captive advisor can sell only a captive product.

The completely independent financial advisor lives on the opposite side of the spectrum. He is free to sell the best investment products available almost anywhere. The exception involves a company-specific product that can be sold only by a company representative. But any other brand of product is an available tool in his toolbox.

Then there is the guy in the middle. He is tied to a company, but not to one company's products. Many fine financial services firms don't have their own products, and thus their agents have access to the same variety of products I can sell.

The difference is in the way they're compensated, which can influence what they sell. A product with the potential for a higher commission might influence an advisor to sell that kind of investment.

Beyond that, because these advisors work for parent companies, they may have benefits — 401(k)s, health insurance, everything employees usually receive. And with those benefits come managers who can influence or even dictate what they sell.

Let's consider an example that illustrates that kind of influence.

Let's say I've sold two investment products, one from Company A and one from Company B. Both generate $100 commissions, meaning I should receive a $200 commission. For an advisor employed by a big-name company, that $200 goes first to the home company, which retains a share of it (for its overhead and expenses) before paying me, say, $80 on one sell and $60 on the other. Instead of a $200 commission, I walk away with only $140. Other than my standard broker-dealer fees, my sales are not being influenced by the broker dealer.

It's the way the company chooses to pay those commissions that can influence which products its agents promote most vigorously. If the company wants to push a particular product for whatever reason, they'll give the advisor a bigger piece of the commission for selling that product. If they prefer that I don't push a particular investment, they'll offer a smaller commission. That influence is more than subtle, as any salesperson's behavior is driven by his compensation.

The bottom line to a client: The investment vehicles sometimes favored by company agents — though perfectly good products — may not be the best available to suit a client's specific needs.

I spent time working as a captive advisor, and although I sold products that made my clients better off than they were previously, today I see a total difference. Being truly independent is like being the general manager of a professional sports team who can pick the best players for his franchise. If a particular player doesn't perform, you replace him with another. That is what a truly independent advisor such as myself does with investments.

Beyond that, I'm also now the owner of my own business, something that is discouraged in the captive world where the home company wants its representatives dependent on the mother ship.

Being independent allows me to grow my company and hire brilliant people so we can do all the things clients truly expect of a full-service financial company. For example, how many financial advisors have their own team of financial plan designers, or have employees dedicated to monitor clients' money, to watch the market and make trades within our own portfolio models? We have that at Affinity Asset Management, which we will describe more fully in Chapter 8.

Moreover, we have the team in place to handle all services — withdrawal requests, financial planning, money management, order processing, client continuing education and outreach — that a client should expect from a good independent financial services company. In working directly for me as opposed to a parent company, my team gives me, the advisor, a better opportunity to work directly with clients to find the financial products that best suit their individual needs.

This is why I'm proud to be a completely independent advisor, one who works directly for the client as opposed to working for the home company. Consider me your personal chief financial officer, your CFO.

Understand how your advisor is compensated

A story about a real client with a fictitious name demonstrates the point I'm making.

Jim Brandis once had all his money with a big-name national company. He liked his financial advisor, who had done a pretty good job of diversifying his investments. And yet, when Jim and I first talked, he had no long-term retirement plan and no tax strategies. Moreover, a lot of his investments were Class A, front-loaded commission products.

Now, front-loaded "A share" mutual funds have their place. Their primary purpose, however, is to pay the expenses of the investment company — as well as the financial advisor who sold the fund — by taking a fee that can be as high as 5.5 percent at the time of sale directly off the top of the investment. When I see a lot of A share holdings in the portfolio of a prospective client, I worry that the person — like too many investors — doesn't understand how advisors get paid, and how that affects their money. [2]

Let's briefly explore this compensation issue.

There are two ways an advisor gets paid — either through commissions or advisory fees. In a commission system, every time I buy something for a client, there's a transaction fee involved that triggers a commission. I get paid, in short, by doing transactions.

---

[2] An explanation of mutual funds, their classes, and associated fees is available at http://www.finra.org/industry/breakpoints-disclosure-statement.

The other way is through an advisory fee, a percentage of the total account value. As the account grows, I get paid more money. If the account value goes down, my revenue goes down.

Clearly, the advisory fee means it's in the advisor's best interest to keep his client's best interest at heart. As the owner of a financial services firm, I know my office rent isn't going down. My employee payroll isn't going down. These costs of business go up every year, meaning I've got to manage accounts that grow. I can't afford to have clients losing large portions of their investments, because that would mean I also lose large parts of my revenue.

A commission-based advisor can sell a product, and what happens to it after the sale doesn't affect his bottom line — at least, not until he tries to sell future products to a disappointed client. But to the advisor working on a percentage of the account's value, making that portfolio perform is as much in his interest as it is in yours. It's like saying an airplane pilot has as much vested interest in landing his plane safely as do his passengers.

Unfortunately, most people don't ask questions about their advisor's limitations in the products he can sell, or how he is paid. They don't know what they don't know.

How a financial advisor gets paid can be determined by multiple factors, and this is something I try to share with clients. I'm very sensitive to not tearing down a client's current financial advisor or what they've done. But what I do try to do is plant small seeds of education and tell people about things I think they may not know.

For instance, I can look at the portfolio of a prospective client and say, "You have some fine investments, but are you aware of the fees in here? Do you know what an A share fund means as opposed to Class B, C or I shares?" I want them to understand that if they deposit $100,000 in a Class A mutual fund with a 4 percent front load, only $96,000 actually gets deposited; the rest is taken off the top in fees compensating the company and the advisor.[3] Remember, too, that front loads may be higher or lower than 4 percent. Many people do know that and say they're fine with it, but I want everyone to understand it in advance.

It's part of the difference in having an advisor who works directly for you.

---

[3] An explanation of mutual funds, their classes, and associated fees is available at http://www.finra.org/industry/breakpoints-disclosure-statement.

CHAPTER 4

Know the rules of a game we all must play

For far too many people, understanding the implications of income taxes on retirement planning — and the strategies to limit those taxes — is like playing a new card game for the first time.

Let's say we're playing cards at your house. It's a game you like and know well, but a new one for me. Who's going to win most immediately in that game? You will, of course, because you know the rules of a game I'm just learning.

But now we've played for an hour, and I'm starting to understand the game better. I begin to win a few hands as the knowledge gap between us diminishes, but I'm still the underdog here. You still have the advantage, because, while I may be learning more about the rules, you still know more about the strategies.

Bottom line, those who know the rules best can develop more effective strategies to use against their opponent. Who's your opponent when it comes to income taxes? The IRS. Let's be clear, we cannot eliminate your income taxes, but with careful planning and implementation of strategies, we can potentially reduce and sometimes drastically reduce those income taxes over your lifetime.

That's why I want to spend these next few chapters explaining the basic rules of how your retirement savings are handled when it comes to taxes. Later, we'll discuss the implications of those rules — how they affect the money you'll be able to save and spend in retirement. Finally, we'll look at some specific strategies to reduce those taxes and better protect the assets you've toiled hard all your working life to amass.

The three buckets

There are all kinds of investment vehicles available to help grow your money. The bottom line, though, is that all those products eventually fall into one of three tax "buckets" — tax deferred, taxable and tax *favorable*. Let's briefly look at the workings of each, then examine their pros and cons.

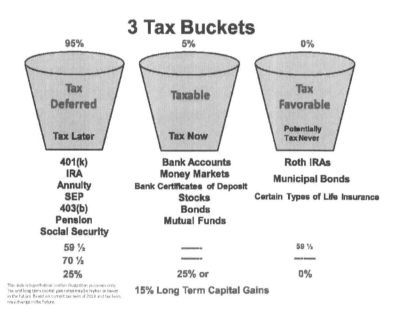

3 Tax Buckets

95%	5%	0%
Tax Deferred	**Taxable**	**Tax Favorable**
Tax Later	Tax Now	Potentially Tax Never
401(k)	Bank Accounts	Roth IRAs
IRA	Money Markets	
Annuity	Bank Certificates of Deposit	Municipal Bonds
SEP	Stocks	
403(b)	Bonds	Certain Types of Life Insurance
Pension	Mutual Funds	
Social Security		
59 ½		59 ½
70 ½		
25%	25% or	0%

This slide is hypothetical and for illustration purposes only. Tax and long term capital gain rates may be higher or lower in the future. Based on current tax laws of 2016 and tax laws may change in the future.

15% Long Term Capital Gains

The tax-deferred — or more correctly, the "tax later" — bucket is the left-hand bucket in the previous illustration.

Here you will find where most people have the greatest chunk of their retirement savings. This is the residing place for 401(k) funds, individual retirement accounts (IRAs), annuities, simplified employee pension plans (SEPs) and 403(b) funds. Your Social Security trust fund and any defined benefit pension — if you're lucky enough to still have one of that vanishing breed — also reside here, growing tax deferred like everything else in this bucket until you begin taking withdrawals, also known as distributions.

Keep in mind that you *WILL* eventually have to begin taking distributions.

Uncle Sam will eventually require you to start taking withdrawals on your qualified money so that you start paying taxes on it. Think about it: The money in retirement plans such as 401(k)s and IRAs has never been taxed. Did you think you would get this break forever? Eventually, the IRS forces us to take distributions that in turn force us to report those withdrawals to the IRS as taxable income. And if you don't follow these rules — if you don't take the distributions and report the income — you will be charged a 50 percent penalty tax on the amount you should have withdrawn. But more on that later.

The middle bucket in the illustration is the "tax now" bucket. These are holdings you pay taxes on now. Included here are bank accounts, money markets, certificates of deposit, stocks, bonds and mutual funds. If your money makes money from interest, dividends or capital gains, you owe taxes annually and get a 1099 at the end of each year.

The right bucket is the tax-*favorable* bucket that includes Roth IRAs, municipal bonds and cash-value life insurance policies. Money invested in these vehicles was taxed as ordinary income before you put it into the Roth, muni bonds or purchased insurance. The growth of *most* money residing here is income tax free. Moreover, *most* withdrawals also are income tax free to you, your surviving spouse or your heirs. [4]

Note the use of the word "most" in the above paragraph. For while it is true that most assets in this bucket grow tax-free and that most distributions can be taken without paying further taxes, there are exceptions. Some municipal bonds, for instance, may be subject to federal AMT taxes or state income taxes, depending on the state or municipality that issues them. Income taken as loans from cash-value life insurance can also be taxed in instances where the policy has lapsed. Exceptions such as these make the conventional "tax free" description of this third bucket less than completely accurate, so we will use "tax favorable" as a more accurate description.

Let's define a few more points before going further.

Most investment vehicles you choose can reside in any of the three buckets. Stocks, bonds and mutual funds — normally middle-bucket investments — can be components of a tax-deferred 401(k) or IRAs. They also can be part of a Roth IRA growing on a tax-*favorable* basis in the right bucket.

Understand, too, that the buckets don't control how an investment will fare, but rather how they are taxed, as well as the rules to that money.

People often mistakenly refer to a Roth IRA as an investment. It is not. A 401(k) is not an investment. Neither is an IRA. Rather, they are tax codes that govern how the investments in each of those accounts are taxed.

To further explain the difference, let's say your stocks, bonds and mutual funds do well and have a gain over a certain period. As a left-bucket holding, under current tax laws you will pay tax on that gain only when you take a withdrawal. In the middle bucket, you pay that tax in the year a gain is realized. *In the right bucket, you*

---

[4] All references to tax buckets and the rules governing them are based on tax law in effect at the writing of this book in 2015.

pay no tax on that growth at all, unless you have one of the exceptions noted before with certain municipal bonds or loans taken against cash-value life insurance policies that have lapsed.

These assets could also lose value equally in all three buckets. But again, the buckets don't make or lose money, the investments in them do.

Those buckets do, however, determine what your tax liability will be at different stages of your life. We'll discuss that briefly here, and in more detail in future chapters.

Pros and cons

Like everything, each bucket has advantages and disadvantages. Let's look at the pros and cons, starting with the positives of each.

Tax-deferred left bucket

The left-bucket vehicle most familiar to many people is the 401(k) in which money is withheld from your paycheck on a pre-tax basis and invested as you direct. You get a tax break right now. If I make $100,000 and put $10,000 into my 401(k), I'm only paying tax on $90,000 that year. That invested money grows, delaying taxes until you make a withdrawal. Moreover, most 401(k)s offer some form of employer matching contribution — free money for retirement. Also growing tax deferred here is your Social Security trust fund into which you paid, as well as any defined benefit pension fund into which your employer contributed. The growth of your Social Security trust fund is not taxed until you start taking withdrawals, at which time a portion of your Social Security may be taxable. Another common transaction here is often done when a person changes jobs and does a rollover of their 401(k) into a traditional IRA. This is a tax-free transaction, as the money remains in the left bucket.

Tax-now middle bucket

The advantage of the middle bucket is that this money is available to you right now, whenever you need it. You're already paying annual taxes on the interest, dividends and capital gains realized here, so the IRS has no restrictions on withdrawals — which is definitely not the case in the left and right buckets. This is your place for liquidity.

Tax-*favorable* right bucket

Albert Einstein said of compound interest that it is, "the eighth wonder of the world. He who understands it, earns it. He who doesn't, pays it." Compound tax-free interest is close behind. Because you've already paid taxes on money invested in right-bucket vehicles, most of the money here — *with the exceptions noted above of some municipal bonds and any loans taken on life insurance policies that have lapsed* — grows and can be withdrawn by you or your heirs on a never-again tax basis under current tax laws.

For every peak there must necessarily be a valley, and each bucket has one or more.

The tax-deferred left bucket is tightly regulated by rules that penalize you for taking money too soon, then again later in life for not taking enough.

We're talking here about the 59 ½ rule and the 70 ½ rule. Most people understand that, with very limited exceptions, you can't withdraw money from your 401(k) or your IRA before age 59 ½. If you do, you not only pay tax on it if it is taxable, but there is also a 10 percent penalty. The rules are there because the IRS wants you to save for your future and really, really doesn't want you touching that money too early.

Beyond that, there is the 70 ½ rule that says you absolutely must start taking distributions on left bucket, tax-deferred money at that age. We're going to examine more closely the effects of the 70 ½ rule on retirement savings in Chapter 5. For right now, though, we'll note in passing that the penalty for not taking RMDs at age 70 ½ is a huge 50 percent of the amount that should have been withdrawn but wasn't. The penalty sting is much more severe than the tax bite here.

We have all been under the age of 59 ½, so most people know at least some part of that rule. But many people under age 70 ½ either have never heard of that rule — probably because it has yet to affect them — or they know of it but choose not to worry about its implications until they reach that age.

Remember, though, that every dollar in this left bucket must someday be drawn and be taxed, whether in your lifetime or after your death. Uncle Sam is the fiddler, and someone must pay him eventually.

The disadvantage to the tax-now middle bucket is obvious. You are paying taxes on these assets every year, and paying more as this bucket grows.

Interest, dividends, capital gains — you get a 1099 on these every year whether you reinvest those proceeds or take them out and spend them. Just as you pay more in taxes as your income grows in your working years, so too must you pay more in income taxes when your invested money makes money.

The tax-favorable right bucket — who doesn't like the sound of that?

The trouble is, very few people have nearly enough of their assets here, and part of that is because they don't fully understand how to get their money into this bucket. The contributions you can make have rules that are largely based on your income. Even if your income qualifies, you're still limited in how much you can save here.

In addition to contributions, you also can make conversions into a Roth IRA, though there is a catch here as well. In Chapter 6 we will illustrate more fully the tax-strategic value of gradually moving assets from the left bucket to the right. But for now, let's merely note that in any left-to-right conversion, you will pay taxes on the money taken from the left, tax-deferred bucket before it converts to the right, tax-favorable bucket, as is done in a Roth IRA conversion.

You pay Uncle Sam now, or pay him later.

There is good news here, however.

A right-bucket Roth IRA does have a 59 ½ rule, though it is less restrictive than the same rule in the left, tax-deferred bucket. There, you can't remove your money under age 59 ½ without penalty. But, because the left and right buckets both have 59 ½ rules, I can move IRA assets from the left to the right bucket at any age without penalty. Moreover, there is no limit to how much I can move in this kind of conversion.

To be sure, I must pay taxes on all money being moved from left to right, but I can make that move whether younger or older than 59 ½. I take what I want to move out of the left bucket, pay taxes on it — but no penalties — then move it into the right bucket, where it continues growing until I or my heirs take distributions, *most of which are taken on a tax-free basis.*

Moreover, I can withdraw some Roth money under age 59 ½ without incurring the major 10 percent penalty of a left-bucket withdrawal.

Here is how that works. Say I put $10,000 into a Roth IRA, and it grows to $12,000. I can touch the $10,000 base — remember, I already paid tax on that money before it entered the right bucket — but I can't touch the $2,000 untaxed growth until age 59 ½. Still, that's an improvement over the limits on my left-bucket assets.

Again, we will illustrate more fully in Chapter 6 the long-range strategy and advantages of left-to-right bucket conversions, especially those made prior to age 70 ½. But for now let's consider a strategy any wage earner can make at any age.[5]

Maximize your 401(k)

I love to hear clients tell me they can invest as much as, say, 15 percent of their paycheck into their retirement account. Investing in yourself cannot be underestimated.

I get a bit concerned, however, when I learn that all of that money has gone into their 401(k), the biggest tax-delayed holding most people have.

Keeping in mind that a cornerstone of our Affinity retirement planning is maximizing your retirement savings, I wonder why more people don't attempt to build up their tax-favorable right-bucket assets that will work to their greater advantage later in life.

As I said at the start of this book, I admire the clients with whom I've been blessed to work. Most have solid financial instincts, a long-term vision and a sense of investing in themselves. Most of them realize that saving 3 to 5 percent of their income today isn't going to pay 100 percent of their income needs in retirement. They know they have to save more. So, they invest 12, maybe 15 percent of their income into their 401(k), and you have to admire their willingness to save.

But sometimes even these good folks need to be shown alternatives.

Let's look at one such hypothetical sound saver, someone with an eye on his future, who might benefit from a restructuring of his retirement contributions during his working years.

---

[5] All references to tax buckets and the rules governing them are based on tax law in effect at the writing of this book in 2015.

Let's say he's making a 15 percent employee contribution each paycheck. He's getting an employer match of 3 percent, bringing his net contribution to 18 percent.

Now let's change the scenario. He's still going to contribute 15 percent, except now he changes his 401(k) contribution to 6 percent — the minimum required to get the 3 percent match from his employer. What does he do with the remaining 9 percent he's ready to invest?

That money goes into his paycheck, still being taxed. Here then is his opportunity to make a Roth IRA investment. He'll pay tax on roughly 2 percent of the remaining 9, leaving him about 7 percent to invest in the Roth *where most of that money will grow without any further taxes until withdrawal under current tax laws*.

Add up the numbers. Putting only 6 percent into his 401(k), getting the 3 percent employer match and putting 7 percent into a Roth gives him a 16 percent net contribution. Not as good, you point out correctly, as his net 18 percent had he put everything in the 401(k).

Well, stand by. Soon I will demonstrate how building up your right-bucket assets, coupled with the tax savings they bring later, after the 70 ½ rules kick into effect, can offset the near-term advantage of tax savings now vs. tax savings later over the long haul.

This is not rocket science. And yet, basic financial strategies like this are simply not being offered to clients by some financial advisors. How do we know this? Time and time again, I meet new clients who, as we work on their plans, tell me ideas such as these have never been fully explained to them by their current advisor.

CHAPTER 5

Pay me now or pay me later

Pay me now or pay me later. We've all heard the expression repeatedly, but it has a special meaning in retirement planning, where the ending part of that phrase often becomes "...or pay me *more* later."

Let me try to illustrate the point.

Let's pretend you're a farmer and I'm the IRS. One day in the early spring I knock on your door and offer you a break on your taxes this year — as if the IRS would ever do that!

But in this fantasy-world example, we'll walk over to your barn here in March, measure what you have in seed, and you can pay tax this year based on the value of that seed. Or, if you prefer, you can plant your seed, grow and harvest your crops, and I'll come back later this summer or fall and you can pay tax on the crops you've grown.

Which do you choose? Would you rather pay tax on your seed now or your crops later?

Truly, it's cheaper to pay tax on the seed than on the harvest. Think of your 401(k) as stored grain that has been growing larger and larger over all these years. All your contributions, all your employer's matches and all the gains in your 401(k) have never been taxed. Eventually, you will have to take this grain to the market, sell it and pay tax.

How does this apply to retirement planning?

Well, you've got a big harvest coming, whether you know it or not. For, at the age of 70 ½, the IRS will literally come knocking on your door demanding that you start taking something called a required minimum distribution, or RMD. It's now time for you to harvest and start paying taxes on the "crops" you've been growing in that left, tax-delayed bucket throughout your working life. Congratulations on your cultivation skills. Your seed is now abundant grain. It's time to pay up.

This is the 70 ½ rule we discussed briefly in Chapter 4, and it never ceases to amaze me how little even my most knowledgeable clients know about its implications.

Most know that something is going to happen at 70 ½. Yet, I'd estimate that less than 2 percent of the people I meet at my seminars know what the penalty is for not taking the distributions on tax-deferred assets that the IRS requires you to take at that age.

What's your guess? What is the penalty if you don't start taking distributions from that left bucket and start paying income taxes on that money?

If you know the penalty to be 50 percent, you've either read up on this or you recall what we mentioned briefly in Chapter 4. Good for you either way.

Yes, you read that right. The IRS will take back half of the money you were supposed to withdraw, and potentially pay income tax on, should you fail to do so. If that doesn't get your attention, nothing will.

The numbers game

Let's break down the impact of this rule with some numbers.

Say your RMD formula, as calculated by the IRS,[6] determines that you have to take $10,000 out of your tax-delayed left bucket in the first year after reaching 70 ½. At a typical 25 percent tax rate, you're paying $2,500 in income taxes on that amount. What you do with the remaining $7,500 is not the concern of the IRS. You can spend it or you can save it in either the taxable or, preferably, the tax-favorable bucket. All the IRS cares is that the money is taken out of that left bucket and it is taxable.

But what if you do nothing? What if you don't take out the $10,000 RMD?

Now instead of paying $2,500 in taxes, you're charged a $5,000 penalty — 50 percent of the $10,000.

What if you take out some, but not the full amount? Say you take out only $8,000 of the $10,000 RMD? At a 25 percent tax rate, you pay $2,000 in income taxes on the $8,000 withdrawal. On the remaining $2,000 you should have taken out but didn't, you pay the 50 percent penalty and lose $1,000. Add it up: On the $8,000 withdrawal you're paying $2,000 in taxes and $1,000 in penalty, a total of $3,000. You'd have been better off taking out the full $10,000 and paying out only $2,500 in taxes.

Keep in mind, the penalty is so big because the IRS wants you to want to pay the tax. And the income tax in this case is the lesser of the two evils.

You probably never dreamed anyone could say that.

It's important to note here that the minimum annual distribution required by the 70 ½ rule is based on two things: a person's age and the size of the qualified assets in the left bucket.

However it is done, you must eventually start tapping that left bucket, whether gradually through your own choosing before age 70 ½, or by an amount determined by the IRS after that. For most

---

[6] IRS rules and formulas for calculating RMDs can be found at http://1.usa.gov/1wdopmC.

people, that's a big bucket to drain, and consequently a big tax burden to bear.

No good deed goes unpunished

The point I'm trying to make is, while your investments are important, it's how you own them — i.e., in which of the three buckets you have them — that is even more important.

With rare exceptions, most people have most of their money in the left and middle buckets. I'd say 95 percent of the people at my workshops have most of their money in the left bucket, which is going to be taxed in the future and is subject to a lot of rules — the only bucket that has both the 59 ½ rules and the 70 ½ rules.

How did it get to be that way?

The government and the financial services industry did a great job in selling the concepts of 401(k)s and IRAs by convincing people that, because they make more money in their earning years, they would have less income and less income tax when they retire. The theory was that, because saving for retirement is a good thing, the government will help you do so by giving you an immediate tax break as a wage earner by reducing your taxable income on the retirement money you invest. Moreover, you might also benefit by possibly paying less income tax when withdrawing that tax-deferred money after retirement when you're not working and likely are in a lower tax bracket.

But we're finding out more and more that this isn't necessarily the case. Many of our clients today say they would like to have a similar lifestyle in retirement, and an income comparable to when they were working. They don't say it, but they're talking about staying in the same tax bracket.

Their situation in retirement, however, has changed considerably from when they were making and saving money in their earning years. Everybody wants to save on taxes, and in your earning years you can take some big deductions on mortgage interest, having kids as deductions, and contributions to your retirement plans.

Now, fast forward to retirement time. Where are your deductions now? You don't have the kids to claim anymore, you're not making contributions to your retirement plan, and your house is probably either paid off or paid down to the point that there's very little or no deduction anymore for mortgage interest. The only major deductions still left to you in retirement are charitable contributions or medical expenses, and you need a lot of those to make it work. Not a good way to take deductions.

Income taxes in retirement suddenly become even more problematic, especially for those who have the bulk of their retirement money in the left bucket, the one requiring taxable withdrawals at 70 ½. Many of our clients tell us the levels of withdrawals they are required to take then are greater than what they need to live on. Because of their Social Security, pensions and other resources, they either don't need their left-bucket income or require very little of it. And yet, because of RMD rules, they end up taking more than they want, thus creating a bigger income and more income taxes at a time when they have few deductions to offset those taxes.

Over the years, I have heard it said that the biggest fear among retirees is running out of money, and that is a big concern for many people. Even though many of our clients have done a good job of saving, this concern about running out of money remains in the back of their minds. Having said that, however, the biggest concern they express to us involves income taxes, the No. 1 complaint I hear from retirees.

It doesn't have to be that way.

I talked in the beginning of this book about what I call the Cornerstone of Affinity. Part of that philosophy is distribution design — an important piece of our company logo. We are talking about making systematic movements of tax-delayed left-bucket assets into tax-now or tax-favorable buckets as a means of reducing incomes taxes in retirement and thus maximizing retirement savings.

In the following chapter, I'll illustrate the advantage of doing so — of paying some tax on the seed today before paying even more on the harvest later.

CHAPTER 6

Stretch out
your retirement savings

What is the biggest concern most people have when facing retirement?

Maintaining good health? A big concern, obviously. Not being a burden to our loved ones? Also huge. Remaining active and living independently with a spouse and friends in a comfortable lifestyle? Sign me up.

Yet the almost universal answer people give when listing their biggest retirement concern is, "Not running out of money if I live a long time."

Figures from the Centers for Disease Control confirm that we are living longer today.[7] As our life expectancy grows, so does our anxiety about whether we saved and invested well enough in our earning years to live a long, independent and comfortable life.

What are the biggest drains on retirement savings? Debt, medical bills and long-term care, inflation and taxes are the biggies. Fortunately, not everyone has debt, not everyone will

---

[7] Larry Copeland. USA Today. Oct. 9, 2014. "Life expectancy in the USA hits a record high." http://www.usatoday.com/story/news/nation/2014/10/08/us-life-expectancy-hits-record-high/16874039/.

incur major medical or long-term care bills, and inflation has remained low for an extended period. But taxes are a constant for everyone and remain one of the single biggest drains on your retirement assets.

Stretching your retirement investments through tax strategies and money management is what I call the *Cornerstone* of Affinity Asset Management. It is both a philosophy and a game plan that helps our company stand out from others with the same goal. In this chapter, we'll use some real-world examples and numbers to break down the components of that philosophy and its implementation.

The $5,000 example

A common goal in any retirement plan is the development of a monthly income stream, funds you know you can count on for however long you live. Social Security is a big part of that plan, but it's usually not enough for most people. Defined-benefit pensions are another income component for a declining number of people — most typically, public service employees still fortunate enough to have such a pension.

For most people, however, their left-bucket, tax-deferred investments — their 401(k)s, IRAs and annuities — coupled with assets in the tax-now bucket (stocks, bonds, mutual funds) will provide the biggest source in filling the hole between what Social Security provides and monthly expenses demand.

Let's look at the tax implications of relying on those two buckets, and what they mean in the work toward making your retirement nest egg last.

$5,000 Example

This is a hypothetical example for a single tax payer

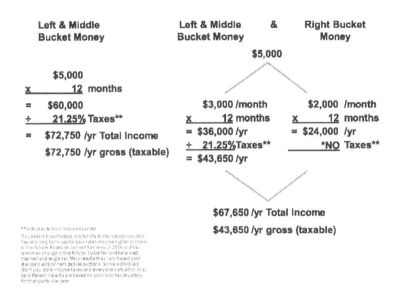

Let's say a person needs $5,000 a month in income, and that money must come from the left or middle buckets because he has very few or no assets in his right, tax-favorable bucket. He takes $5,000 a month multiplied by 12 months — $60,000 annually taken from taxable assets. But the counting isn't over. Because this money was taken from tax-deferred or tax-now sources, *this taxpayer, who in 2015 would be paying a 21.25 percent tax rate, needs to take out a total of $72,750 — upon which he'll pay $12,750 in taxes — in order to net $60,000 a year and the $5,000 a month he needs.* [8]

Now, let's look at an alternate way to achieve the same goal.

---

[8] To be fair and balanced; married and single tax filers results may vary based your standard and/or itemized deductions. Some individuals don't pay state income taxes and everyone's situation may be different. Results are based on your own tax situation for that particular year.

We still have the $5,000 monthly need, only this time we'll tap different sources. This time, we will take only $3,000 a month from the left and middle buckets. Multiply that by 12 months, $36,000. *When taxes are factored in, our single taxpayer, paying taxes at a 21.25 percent rate, will have to withdraw a total of $43,650 — on which $7,650 represents taxes — in order to net $36,000 a year and his $3,000 monthly goal.*

We are, of course, still $2,000 short of our monthly goal of $5,000. So, in this second example we're going to take that missing $2,000 from the right, tax-favorable bucket of Roth IRAs, municipal bonds or cash-value life insurance. That's $2,000 a month times 12 months, equaling $24,000, but this time with no tax involved — *in all but a few situations* — under current tax law. *Add the $24,000 in right bucket withdrawals to the $43,650 in taxed distributions, this time the client's total withdrawal is $67,650 a year.*

Again, in both examples the client is taking $5,000 per month from his retirement assets. *But he's now saving $5,100 annually — the difference between $72,750 and $67,650* — just by taking some of his monthly income from the tax-favorable buckets we've been encouraging him to build up over the years.

Our goal at Affinity Asset Management is to design a retirement plan to create the biggest net income, or the least gross income that is taxable income. Again, saving on taxes means more money for you to spend or grow in retirement.

The bottom line is obvious. Your retirement nest egg is going to last longer if you spend less on taxes. For that to happen, however, you will have to change your strategy now that you've become more familiar with the rules of the game.

Don't wait until age 70 ½

I've come to believe there are two common mistakes people make in retirement planning.

One is that they leave their retirement income untouched for too long, only to find they encounter problems at age 70 ½. Even the people who know about the rules regarding required minimum distributions at that age too often have the mentality of, "I'll deal with it when I get there." Those who plan ahead, however, can realize a dramatic snowball effect in the way their tax savings can roll up.

Flip the page to see the charts illustrating this point.

Both of the accompanying examples start with a $500,000 balance in the 401(k) or IRA of a 62-year-old man with a wife the same age. For illustration purposes, both examples assume an average growth rate in his left-bucket assets of 8 percent a year.

In the first chart, the gentleman takes no distributions from age 62 through 69. He is not required to do so, and because he perhaps has other resources — a job, a pension or other income on which he and his wife can live — or because he doesn't yet want to pay income tax on his 401(k) or IRA withdrawals, he chooses to leave his tax-deferred assets untouched for as long as he can.

But now he reaches age 70 ½. His IRA balance has grown to almost $925,500, and now he is required to take a minimum first-year distribution of $33,776 taxable dollars. That RMD will rise in subsequent years: $36,340 at age 71, $39,094 at 72, and up and up. That's income he'll have to pay taxes on in addition to his Social Security, pension, investment earnings and other middle-bucket income, as well as part-time wages and any other regular income.

By the time he reaches age 90, he has a yearly RMD of $121,595. His combined taxable distributions just from those 401(k) and IRA accounts after 20 years stand at a little more than $1.5 million.

Example 1

Husband - 62 years old Wife - 62 years old IRA Balance - $500,000 Growth Rate - 8%					
Year	Age	Balance	Life Exp.	Distribution	Total Distribution
2007	62	$500,000.00	23.5	$0.00	$0.00
2008	63	$540,000.00	22.7	$0.00	$0.00
2009	64	$583,200.00	21.8	$0.00	$0.00
2010	65	$629,856.00	21	$0.00	$0.00
2011	66	$680,224.00	20.2	$0.00	$0.00
2012	67	$734,664.04	19.4	$0.00	$0.00
2013	68	$793,437.16	18.6	$0.00	$0.00
2014	69	$856,912.13	17.8	$0.00	$0.00
2015	70	$925,465.10	27.4	$33,776.10	$33,776.10
2016	71	$963,024.12	26.5	$36,340.53	$70,116.63
2017	72	$1,000,818.28	25.6	$39,094.46	$109,211.09
2018	73	$1,038,661.73	24.7	$42,051.08	$151,262.17
2019	74	$1,086,339.50	23.8	$45,224.35	$196,486.52
2020	75	$1,113,604.36	22.9	$48,629.01	$245,115.53
2021	76	$1,150,173.38	22	$52,280.61	$297,396.14
2022	77	$1,185,724.19	21.2	$55,930.39	$353,326.53
2023	78	$1,220,177.30	20.3	$60,107.26	$413,433.79
2024	79	$1,252,875.64	19.5	$64,250.03	$477,683.82
2025	80	$1,283,715.66	18.7	$68,647.90	$546,331.72
2026	81	$1,312,273.18	17.9	$73,311.35	$619,643.07
2027	82	$1,338,078.78	17.1	$78,250.22	$697,893.29
2028	83	$1,360,614.84	16.3	$83,473.30	$781,366.59
2029	84	$1,379,312.86	15.5	$88,987.93	$870,354.52
2030	85	$1,393,550.92	14.8	$94,158.85	$964,513.37
2031	86	$1,403,343.44	14.1	$99,527.90	$1,064,041.27
2032	87	$1,408,120.78	13.4	$105,083.64	$1,169,124.91
2033	88	$1,407,280.11	9.7	$110,809.46	$1,279,934.37
2034	89	$1,400,188.30	9.1	$116,682.36	$1,396,616.73
2035	90	$1,386,186.42	11.4	$121,595.30	$1,518,212.03
2036	91	$1,365,758.41	10.8	$126,459.11	$1,644,671.14
2037	92	$1,338,443.24	10.2	$131,219.93	$1,775,891.07
2038	93	$1,303,801.17	9.6	$135,812.62	$1,911,703.69
2039	94	$1,261,427.63	9.1	$138,618.42	$2,050,322.11
2040	95	$1,212,633.95	8.6	$141,003.95	$2,191,326.06
2041	96	$1,157,360.40	8.1	$142,884.00	$2,334,210.06
2042	97	$1,095,634.51	7.6	$144,162.44	$2,478,372.50

Pension Distribution Calculator

This slide is hypothetical and for illustration purposes only. Tax and long term capital gain rates may be higher or lower in the future. Life expectancies are based on tables in 2015 and may change in the future.

Example 2

Husband - 62 years old Wife - 62 years old IRA Balance - $500,000 Growth Rate - 8%					
Year	Age	Balance	Life Exp.	Distribution	Total Distribution
2007	62	$500,000.00	23.5	$37,500.00	$37,500.00
2008	63	$499,500.00	22.7	$37,500.00	$75,500.00
2009	64	$498,960.00	21.8	$37,500.00	$112,500.00
2010	65	$498,376.80	21	$37,500.00	$150,000.00
2011	66	$497,746.94	20.2	$37,500.00	$187,500.00
2012	67	$497,066.70	19.4	$37,500.00	$225,000.00
2013	68	$496,332.04	18.6	$37,500.00	$262,500.00
2014	69	$495,538.60	17.8	$37,500.00	$300,000.00
2015	70	$494,681.39	27.4	$37,500.00	$337,500.00
2016	71	$493,756.23	26.5	$37,500.00	$375,500.00
2017	72	$492,756.73	25.6	$37,500.00	$412,500.00
2018	73	$491,677.27	24.7	$37,500.00	$450,000.00
2019	74	$490,511.45	23.8	$37,500.00	$487,500.00
2020	75	$489,252.37	22.9	$37,500.00	$525,000.00
2021	76	$487,892.56	22	$37,500.00	$562,500.00
2022	77	$486,423.96	21.2	$37,500.00	$600,000.00
2023	78	$484,937.88	20.3	$37,500.00	$637,500.00
2024	79	$483,124.91	19.5	$37,500.00	$675,000.00
2025	80	$481,274.90	18.7	$37,500.00	$712,500.00
2026	81	$479,276.89	17.9	$37,500.00	$750,000.00
2027	82	$477,119.04	17.1	$37,500.00	$787,500.00
2028	83	$474,788.56	16.3	$37,500.00	$825,000.00
2029	84	$472,271.64	15.5	$37,500.00	$862,500.00
2030	85	$469,553.37	14.8	$37,500.00	$900,000.00
2031	86	$466,617.64	14.1	$37,500.00	$937,500.00
2032	87	$463,447.05	13.4	$37,500.00	$975,000.00
2033	88	$460,022.81	12.7	$37,500.00	$1,012,500.00
2034	89	$456,324.63	12	$38,027.05	$1,050,527.05
2035	90	$451,761.39	11.4	$39,628.19	$1,090,155.24
2036	91	$445,103.86	10.8	$41,213.32	$1,131,368.56
2037	92	$436,201.78	10.2	$42,764.88	$1,174,133.44
2038	93	$424,911.85	9.6	$44,261.65	$1,218,395.09
2039	94	$411,102.22	9.1	$45,176.07	$1,263,571.16
2040	95	$395,200.24	8.6	$45,953.52	$1,309,524.68
2041	96	$377,186.46	8.1	$46,566.23	$1,356,090.91
2042	97	$357,069.85	7.6	$46,982.88	$1,403,073.79

Pension Distribution Calculator

This slide is hypothetical and for illustration purposes only.
Tax and long term capital gain rates may be higher or lower
in the future. Life expectancies are based on tables in 2015
and may change in the future.

Now let's look at the second example for the same man, same 401(k)/IRA, same rate of return, but who has followed our recommendations.

Instead of taking no distributions until required to do so, this gentleman starts taking an annual withdrawal of $37,500 at age 62. Because he's reducing his left-bucket, tax-deferred pool, he's able to continue taking that same $37,500 annual distribution until it finally goes up marginally to $38,027 at age 89. His withdrawal rate over 27 years remained level, as did the taxes he paid on those withdrawals. When he is 90, his total taxable distributions are just under $1.1 million.

Admittedly, in taking that $37,500 distribution for eight years before he was required to do so, this gentleman paid taxes on that money in each of those years. But consider the savings over his lifetime.

The gentleman in our first example, who did no tax planning and took no withdrawals until he had to, has paid taxes on $1.5 million in total required distributions at age 90. The second client, who took steady withdrawals since age 62, has paid taxes on only $1.1 million at the same age. That's a $400,000 difference that, at our mythical 25 percent tax rate, means the second man saved $100,000 in income tax over the years just by knowing the rules of his money.

Now ask yourself this question: What is more important to me? Saving the most on income taxes this year, or saving the most on income taxes over my lifetime? Most people would choose savings over a lifetime.

Look at it another way. Imagine you just won the lottery — Congratulations! — and you have a big check coming. You know you'll have to pay income tax on those winnings at some time. Do you take your winnings in a one-time payment, with a big chunk deducted immediately for taxes? Or, do you take your winnings in a steady income stream spread out over multiple years, with a reduced tax burden each year?

It's easy for all of us to walk around with blinders on and focus only on immediate benefits and instant gratification. But those who know the rules to their money acquire the vision to develop income tax reduction strategies that ultimately give you more money to spend — or more to grow.

At Affinity we believe in leveling out that tax burden over time. In the above example, for instance, we spread the tax burden for the second client, the one taking distributions each year from age 62, over 28 years as opposed to 20 for the man who took nothing until he had to do so at age 70 ½. Doing that saved the second man $100,000 in income taxes over the course of his retirement. That's an extra $100,000 he had available to spend or save.

Once again, the best way to achieve that saving is by slowly reducing your tax-deferred holdings — a little each year — and building up your tax-favorable assets before you are required to start draining that left bucket at 70 ½. Paying a little on taxes now, when moving money from the left to right bucket, can mean larger lifetime tax savings. It's why we encourage clients to start these strategies as soon as we meet them, regardless of age.

One final note on the example above. Some sharp-eyed readers will note correctly that the first man who took no distributions until required to do so has an IRA balance at age 90 of almost $1.4 million — roughly three times that of the second man's $452,000 balance at the same age.

Keep in mind, however, that nobody said the second man spent the money he began to withdraw at age 62. If he followed our recommendations, he took left-bucket money from his 401(k) or IRA each year, paid taxes on it, then converted part or all of it into a right-bucket Roth IRA where it continued to grow until he or his beneficiaries are ready to take tax-free withdrawals.

Remember, too, that the same kind of investments the man had in the left bucket can be used after converting funds into the right. If he was enjoying an 8 percent return in the tax-deferred bucket, there is no reason he can't realize the same return in tax-favorable growth.

In short, the total balance in his left and right buckets could be comparable to the left-bucket balance of the man who took no distributions. If you factor in tax savings, the second man fares even better in the big picture.

In building financial plans for clients using these tax strategies and retirement income strategies, we find the typical client's income goes up each year for inflationary reasons even as they maintain a level tax rate. Yes, it's like creating your own personal flat tax.

Moreover, we also find we are able to create increasing incomes with a decreasing income tax rate. Of course, we all want increasing income and decreasing taxes. The difference depends on each client's situation; everyone is different. Age, retirement timeline, amount saved and amount grown all play a part.

Don't ignore the tax strategies

I said earlier there were two mistakes most commonly made in retirement planning.

The second, which dovetails on the one described above, is the failure to employ the simple tax strategies that can achieve significant savings over a hopefully long and comfortable retirement.

I'm talking here about something as simple as building up your right-bucket assets. This can be difficult for people who don't like paying income taxes now, despite the knowledge that they could realize a tax saving in retirement.

I understand that thinking. What you must understand, however, is the ultimate value you — or your surviving spouse or heirs — will realize further down the road.

Growing your money wisely, and in a way that will give you the greatest tax saving, is our goal at Affinity Asset Management.

To do that, we want your money growing in all three buckets. The three do not have to be in perfect balance — indeed, they probably never will be. You will likely never get all your tax-deferred money out of the left bucket, but if we can slowly and systematically get a sizable amount of it moved into the right bucket, the tax-favorable advantages later in life will be more than worth the effort.

Our goal is to create a strategy for gradual conversions, which — unlike the rules that limit the contributions you can make — have no restrictions on how much you can move into the right bucket as long as it's coming from that left bucket. Each plan we build is unique to the client, depending on age, assets, special needs and time frame.

The long-range value here is in flattening out the RMD rate you will face at 70 ½. Instead of having it rise every year as you get older, you can keep it flat by controlling the left-bucket money the IRS finally gets to access. When your withdrawal rate is flat, so, too, are your taxes.

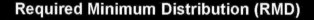

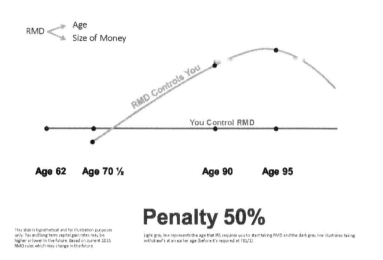

How early is too early to start doing this? How late is too late? The sooner in life you can do it, the better. It's really ideal for people under 70. You can do it when you're beyond that, but it doesn't have as much value then as the rules change slightly on how much you can convert.

One more note on left-to-right bucket Roth conversions.

We always do them at the end of the year, for two reasons. One, by paying at the end of the year, you don't give the IRS your money any earlier than you have to. As opposed to contributions that can be made until April 15 of the following year, a Roth conversion has to be made in the calendar year, with a Dec. 31 deadline, so we usually do them in November or December.

The other reason for end-of-year conversions is that it gives us the opportunity to look back on the year, reevaluate the blueprint we drew up and see if changes need to be made. Did something happen in the past year that changes the amount of the conversion we had planned, either up or down? We might even find we need to skip a conversion that year. But it's good to look back at the entire year before we actually do the conversion. Doing something early in a year means there is a lot of time, a lot of things that can happen, to affect your tax situation.

Think of your heirs

Our tax strategies have three principle benefits.

One is to save on income taxes for Mom and Dad, or a husband and wife, while they are alive.

The second is to save on income taxes for the survivor in the couple. One will outlive the other and will probably inherit the sum of the money. But the survivor will now file a single person's tax return, and single people pay more in taxes than married people. By inheriting more right-bucket, tax-favorable money, however, the survivor will pay less in income taxes.

Let me cite an example.

I knew a retired couple making about $100,000 in annual retirement income. One died and the income for the other fell to about $80,000 through a $20,000 decrease in Social Security.

They agreed while both were alive that an $80,000 income for the survivor would be just fine. But what they didn't realize was the single person would pay more in tax on the $80,000 than they both did combined on the $100,000.[9] That shocked them when we talked about what happens when people become single (not by choice). The surviving spouse inherits the deceased spouse's money, they have to deal with rising RMDs, and they must do all this while paying increased income taxes as a single person. Ouch!

The third major advantage of our tax strategies involves the couple's heirs, who will fare better if they inherit more tax-

---

[9] All references to tax buckets and the rules governing them are based on tax law in effect at the writing of this book in 2015.

favorable assets. Because they will pay less in income taxes, they net a bigger inheritance.

Almost everything in the middle and right buckets is inherited free of income tax. The only inheritance heirs must pay income taxes on, for the most part, are assets in the left bucket — the biggest piece of most estates.

One last story here.

We had a client couple with whom we worked. Mom died in 2013, and Dad passed a year later after a battle with bad health. We also had their children as clients. They knew they were going to inherit money soon, and that there were income taxes to be paid on IRA money their folks still had. Someone was going to have to pay it, either the parents now or the kids later.

It was decided that, because the parents' medical bills were so high late in life, they had enough in deductions and their income was low enough that they elected to do a really large conversion from their IRA left-bucket money to a Roth IRA right bucket.

The kids still inherited some left bucket money they had to pay income tax on, but, because there was less of it, they netted a bigger inheritance. They loved us for the ideas we provided for them and their parents. We didn't change any of their investments, but moved $100,000 in those same investments into the right bucket.

Dad's decision to pay those taxes proved to be his final gift to his children.

CHAPTER 7

It's not enough to win on paper

Let's take a quick pop quiz. Don't worry, this won't count on your final grade.

Say you invested $10, and after a couple months of solid performance that investment is now worth $15. How much did you make?

If you said $5, you missed an important element of the trick question.

Let's try again. Let's say that same $10 investment didn't perform well, its value falling to $8. How much did you lose?

If you now know that you haven't lost anything just yet, you've caught on to the point I'm trying to make.

The answer is, you never really made $5 on the positive return, or lost $2 on the negative return, until you sell the investment and lock in the gain or loss. Knowing when and how to sell is critical in the world of investing.

Sadly, too many people in retirement don't fully appreciate how selling assets they spent a lifetime amassing affects their savings nest egg. The proper harvesting of the crop they've grown — that is, turning investment money into regular monthly retirement income — is almost as important as was the proper planting of the seeds all those many years ago.

Let's add another component to our pop quiz to illustrate the point.

Say you gave me $20, and I put $10 in one investment and $10 in another. One grows to $15, the other falls to $8. Now it comes time to take a $2 withdrawal — in retirement, for instance. Do I take that $2 from the $15 investment or the $8 one?

Most people attending the seminars I give say they would take the withdrawal from the under-performing $8 investment as opposed to the $15 investment that is producing nicely. It's a common sense answer, but not the right one.

Remembering that you don't make or lose money until you sell an asset, isn't it preferable to lock in a $2 gain instead of a $2 loss? If I take $2 out of the investment that grew to $15, it's still worth $13 — still a gain in your holdings. If I take $2 from the investment that fell to $8, it's now worth $6.

Take that example one step further. Again, we've split your $20 investment into two parts, and this time both did well. One $10 investment is at $15 and the other $10 investment is at $13. Now where do I take my $2 withdrawal? The answer is the same as before — you generally take from the top producers.

It is a financial fact of life that not all our investments will be home runs, or even infield singles. We've all had bad investments. But even one that starts out bad can eventually get better later. Conversely, a good investment now can eventually turn sour. That's why it's important to do a good job during the "planting" process of diversifying your investments, knowing some will perform better than others. Some will grow, some will remain flat, some will even lose. On average, however, the gains of a well-diversified portfolio should outweigh the losses.

But it's equally importation to diversify when harvesting the gains of your retirement savings.

This is why distribution design is a key fourth element of our Affinity Asset Management logo. Making smart, timely withdrawals in retirement is a major component in helping make the most of your retirement savings. The example below illustrates this point.

The difference Bill could have made

We met Bill, the client whose investments are illustrated in the graphs accompanying this chapter, just after his third year of retirement. He was doing well in that time, but he came to us to see if he could do better.

In our analysis of his first years of retirement, things looked good on the surface. His investments were growing, he had good income flowing into his bank account every month from his investment account (IRAs), he had a good relationship with his financial advisor who put him in some good investments, and his accounts were growing more than what he was taking out to live on. What more could he want?

Well, how about a $10,000 improvement in the balance of his IRA over that same three-year period?

Let's look at how we were able to make the improvement with the charts on the following pages.

Bill's initial plan – monthly withdrawals

FUND	2004	2005	2006	Income Taken - Monthly
Investment A	9%	6%	8%	$0
Investment B	18%	14%	21%	$0
Investment C	16%	4%	21%	$0
Investment D	13%	42%	12%	$800
Investment E	18%	10%	20%	$1,300
Investment F	12%	9%	18%	$900
Investment G	15%	12%	21%	$500
Investment H	18%	17%	23%	$0
Investment I	12%	6%	20%	$800
Investment J	14%	11%	15%	0
Investment K	0%	1%	3%	$0

Total Amount taken annually $51,600

IRA Rollover (Beginning Value)   **$590,915**
Ending Market Value   **$647,089**

This example is an actual client that came to Mark in 2007. The client had retired in December of 2003. These slides show the importance of taking withdraws and choosing the right place to take the withdraws. Additionally, this works well because these years were all positive returns which really drives the point home that even with positive returns you still need to make good decisions about where you take the monthly withdraws.

This slide is hypothetical and for illustration purposes only. Tax and long term capital gain rates may be higher or lower in the future.

Securities and Advisory Services offered through Client One Securities, LLC Member FINRA/SIPC, and an Investment Advisor Affinity Asset Management and Client One Securities, LLC are not affiliated.

Bill's new plan – annual totals

FUND	2004	2005	2006	Income Taken Annually - 2004	Income Taken Annually - 2005	Income Taken Annually - 2006
Investment A	9%	6%	8%	$0	$0	$0
Investment B	18%	14%	21%	$10,000	$10,000	$7,000
Investment C	16%	4%	21%	$11,000	$0	$11,000
Investment D	13%	42%	12%	$0	$7,000	$0
Investment E	18%	10%	20%	$9,000	$0	$10,000
Investment F	12%	9%	18%	$0	$0	$0
Investment G	15%	12%	21%	$7,000	$6,000	$7,000
Investment H	18%	17%	23%	$0	$0	$0
Investment I	12%	6%	20%	$0	$0	$0
Investment J	14%	11%	15%	$0	$0	$0
Investment K	0%	1%	3%	$14,600	$28,600	$16,600

Total Amount taken annually $51,600 $51,600 $51,600

IRA Rollover (Beginning Value) $590,915
Ending Market Value $657,329

This slide is hypothetical and for illustration purposes only. Tax and long term capital gain rates may be higher or lower in the future.

Upon retirement, Bill had rolled nearly $591,000 from his 401(k) into a personal IRA — a tax-free rollover — with a major national financial service company. His financial advisor diversified that money into 11 different investments, all of which experienced positive returns in each of his first three years of retirement. Bill took a monthly withdrawal of $4,300 from that IRA, or $51,600 a year. With that money from his IRA account, and Social Security for himself and his wife, they made about $80,000 a year — a good, comfortable retirement income.

Bill's monthly withdrawals from his IRA to his bank account were determined by his financial advisor. The advisor set up the IRA accounts to take withdrawals from five of the investments inside the IRA each month — the same amount every month. He took the biggest chunk, $1,300, of that monthly $4,300 from one of his best-producing investments (fund E), but left untouched the assets in two others (B and H) also at the top of his performance list.

Three years later, Bill has withdrawn just under $155,000 in assets, yet his IRA balance has grown to just over $647,000 because of the good returns. Who wouldn't want a portfolio that looks like this?

And yet, things could have been better had his advisor simply put some human brain power into his withdrawal strategies. That's what we did in looking at different ways of generating the same monthly income while demonstrating how we could produce a better end result just by selling his assets differently.

The practice of withdrawing the same amount from the same investments each period is called "dollar-cost averaging out." It's the same concept as the familiar dollar-cost averaging approach to investing money, only on a reverse basis.

I don't like doing dollar-cost averaging out. I call it the lazy financial advisor's way. Here's why.

Most people understand the advisability of selling at the right time — the second essential component of "buy low, sell high." Yet, the computer making Bill's automatic withdrawals on, say, the 20th of every month has no idea whether that day is a good day or a bad day to sell on the market. It only knows it is programmed to make a certain amount in withdrawals on a specific date each month, as well as the five funds from which to take those withdrawals.

I much prefer the human touch of a financial advisor who can look at the performance of individual investments inside a retirement portfolio and then select what should be sold to most efficiently generate whatever monthly income stream the client needs.

The second chart shows the distribution design model we prepared for Bill's IRA.

Note that our recommended withdrawals tapped two of his top three most productive investments (B and E), while leaving another hot producer (investment H) alone. Note, too, that we mined our single biggest chunks of money in each of the three years from Bill's lowest producing asset (investment K). This was a money-market fund with way too much cash that was making Bill next to nothing in a low-to-no interest market. Why not take money from this source while letting the others grow?

Reducing a large holding in cash or conservative money markets is often an option to consider. While this money is certainly safe, it also is what I call "unemployed money," in that it returns next to nothing in a low- or no-interest environment. To be sure, we do keep a certain amount in cash for clients as a safety net. But Bill had too much, so we used part of that cash as a source for withdrawals while also taking withdrawals from his more productive accounts.

Note also that the withdrawals from Bill's IRA in our model were taken on an annual basis, as opposed to the computer's monthly withdrawals. No human has the time to do that for each client each month.

What we can and will do, however, is periodically look at all investments in a client's retirement portfolio and take three, six or 12 months' worth of withdrawals, picking and choosing the most strategic investments to sell at those intervals. Proceeds from the assets' sales go into the client's money market account, from which he draws a monthly income.

In Bill's case, we identified on a yearly basis those investments we wanted to sell to generate 12 months of income. Over a three-year period, we sold investments only three times to create three 12-month income blocks. Bill still got the monthly income he wanted. The only difference was that human brain power was employed to analyze his investments and determine the best source from which to take withdrawals.

The end result?

Doing things the computer's way, Bill's account that started at almost $591,000 had a balance of just over $647,000 — despite taking nearly $155,000 in withdrawals — after three years. Not bad. But after back-testing the recommendations in our model, we determined that Bill would have had a balance exceeding $657,000 — a $10,000 difference after three years. [10]

---

[10] "Back testing" refers to a process in which we use computer software (a Morningstar program at our company) to input a mix of investments to see how that mix would have performed in a historical context.. We can test the rate of return, alphas, betas, standard deviation and fees.

Obviously, we don't have a crystal ball, so we don't know where the market is going. Back testing allows us to see how a group of investments worked together. Not all investments will grow equally. Some will grow, some will be flat, some will lose. When put together using various market sectors and industries as well as the right combination of U.S. stocks and international stocks, along with a stocks vs. bonds blend, we can see with back testing how this combination would have performed. Back testing gives us a baseline on which to create our seven investment models.

What This Means To You

	IRA Rollover (Beginning Value)	Ending Market Value
Income Taken Monthly	$590,915	$647,089
Income Taken Annually	$590,915	$657,329
Difference	$0	**$10,240**

This difference represents the two ending market value's over 3 years.

This slide is hypothetical and for illustration purposes only.
Tax and long term capital gain rates may be higher or lower in the future.

Securities and Advisory Services offered through Client One Securities, LLC Member FINRA/SIPC,
and an Investment Advisor Affinity Asset Management and Client One Securities, LLC are not affiliated

Same investments, same rate of return, same withdrawal rate. The only difference was that we manually picked where to take the withdrawals versus the computer's systematic "dollar-cost averaging out."

Bottom line, Bill had been getting good investment advice.

His advisor with the major financial services company had given him good advice about diversification, which everyone wants. Monthly income was being deposited into his bank account in retirement, which everyone wants. His account continued to grow even after taking those withdrawals, which everyone wants. He had a good relationship with his advisor, who was continuing to make periodic reviews and kept Bill informed, which everyone wants.

But what he wasn't getting was good withdrawal advice.

The biggest reason for saving money when we are younger is to spend it as needed in retirement. Well, you can't spend it until you sell off some of those investments, and doing that in the way that works to your best advantage is what wasn't being done in Bill's case. He didn't even know what he was missing in the selling/distribution process set up by his advisor.

Again, as investors we expect certain services from our advisors, but most of the time we don't really know if we are getting them. The way most of our clients learn about what they've been missing is when they come to see us for the first time and we analyze their situation and formulate a plan.

Truly, withdrawals are way too important to not get the full attention of your financial advisor. It's why distribution design represents one-quarter of the puzzle in our company logo.

I ask again: Why haven't I heard this before?

Let's be frank here.

Financial advisors get paid to sell, not to make withdrawals. In all my 19 years in this industry and in my work with lots of different companies, never once had I been trained on the best way to make withdrawals. Those companies trained me and paid me to sell their products, and to grow those products. But they never trained me on the best way to take withdrawals.

Why is that? Short answer, withdrawals don't make any money for an insurance company, or an investment company, or a bank.

I can't emphasize this enough. The No. 1 reason we make investments with money taken from our paychecks during our working years is to save for retirement. But you can't spend that money until you sell pieces of your investments, bit-by-bit, and create the income that replaces your paycheck in retirement. Until your advisor triggers a sale that turns part of your investments into cash that is electronically transferred to your bank account for you to live on, your retirement savings are like the $10 investment example cited at the beginning of this chapter. It is neither a gain nor a loss until you cash in.

Knowing the best way to sell an investment — or when to get out of it completely — is an essential part of financial planning. It is different than knowing how to make investments. That's why it amazes me that not enough people in this business get trained on the best way to liquidate investments when it comes time to put money in a client's bank account. I hear that sentiment expressed often in talks I give to other financial advisors.

Keep in mind here that I'm not talking about having some kind of crystal ball when it comes to market timing. We don't know when the stock market will go up or down any more than you do.

What we do know is this: In reviewing your retirement investments, when we see a $10 investment — again, as in the example above — that is now worth $15, it is not enough to have a $5 gain merely on paper. Selling a part of that investment at the right time is essential to locking in a gain and turning it into income you can live on. Selling an investment from your taxable bucket at a loss is something to consider only if you need to offset a gain for tax purposes. However, since most people have the majority of their money in the left, tax-deferred bucket, selling a loss to offset a gain in this bucket is not commonly done since there is no tax advantage to doing this from the left bucket.

One other important note here.

Don't forget to see the big picture when planning your withdrawals. Even before considering from which individual investments to take your withdrawals, make sure you and your financial advisor first discuss the buckets you will tap. Drawing from investments in the correct buckets is a big part of the Affinity distribution design. Our models likely won't draw income from any one bucket, but rather from all three — depending on a person's age and needs, of course.

For instance, a person early in retirement at age 62 could do better — as illustrated in the previous chapter — to take withdrawals from investments in his left and middle buckets while letting his right bucket assets grow for the tax savings they will generate after the 70 ½ rules kick in.

CHAPTER 8

Who's looking out for your money?

I knew a long time ago that if we were to grow my Affinity Asset Management company, we were going to have to do things different than a typical financial advisor might do.

Looking back, this was a great decision. How do I know? Because I have done countless public speaking engagements over the years in front of the general public as well as other financial advisors. The general public would ask questions and tell me stories about their current advisors and what they were doing or not doing. I also would hear from financial advisors in my audience who talked about how they did things. I soon came to believe that many advisors have very few or no systems in place to watch and manage their clients' money.

One of the things we do different at Affinity is advocating tax minimization strategies.[11] Another is our distribution design. And a third key difference is the way we manage the assets our clients have entrusted to us.

---

[11] To be clear, we advocate tax minimization strategies, but we do not give specific tax advice at Affinity Asset Management.

I've always believed people should not judge their financial advisor just on the products he or she sells. They also should judge their advisor on how he or she manages those products after they make the sale.

Money management involves more than just the products that are sold today. A client's life is going to change over time, meaning we as advisors have to change their asset allocations from time to time to stay current with what's going on with each client and the economic world around them.

Keeping up with the impact of global economics is difficult for the average investor who understandably is more interested in what is happening locally. That is, in his own state, in his community and — most importantly — in his own life. During our client reviews, people are good about keeping us informed about changes going on in their lives. But not nearly enough know what we know about global concerns, the state of the economy or the stock market. It's the job of an active money manager to make the necessary changes to their accounts when things happen in the world to affect their money.

The macro world ultimately has a direct influence on the micro world of our investors, who care mainly about the bottom line performance of their investments. That's why we as financial advisors must stay on top of the big picture to make sure we are moving our clients in the right direction.

Money management models

To do that, we created our own set of seven investment models at Affinity. Similar in structure to those employed by the big national companies, each contains a varied mix of stocks and bonds that range in risk/return levels from conservative (our model 1) to aggressive (model 7).

The Affinity difference? Our money management models are developed locally, with our own people doing the market analysis and investment research, placing trades, back-testing the performance of each model,[12] monitoring current economic conditions and changing investments within each model as needed.

Our models are never stagnant in their stocks-to-bonds combination. They vary depending on the economy. Our middle model, No. 3, had a 68 percent stock/30 percent bond and 2 percent cash mix in early 2015 when stocks were outperforming bonds. But just a few years previously, that same No. 3 model was a 50-50 combination at a time when bonds were performing higher. Note also that, when we adjust one model, we adjust all seven.

These models best help us manage risk. Let's say one of the investments in the model performs very well, or let's say it becomes a non-performer. When we need to do something with any investment — buy more of it, sell some of it, get out of it completely — we can make those changes quickly to the advantage of all clients in each of those models.

It's all about managing performance and making sure we have funds at the top of the rankings in there. When something that was the best investment at one time is no longer the best, we

---

[12] "Back testing" refers to a process in which we use computer software (a Morningstar program at our company) to input a mix of investments to see how that mix would have performed in a historical context. We can test the rate of return, alphas, betas, standard deviation and fees.

Obviously, we don't have a crystal ball, so we don't know where the market is going. Back testing allows us to see how a group of investments worked together. Not all investments will grow equally. Some will grow, some will be flat, some will lose. When put together using various market sectors and industries as well as the right combination of U.S. stocks and international stocks, along with a stocks vs. bonds blend, we can see with back testing how this combination would have performed. Back testing gives us a baseline on which to create our seven investment models.

replace it with something better. When an A student becomes a B-plus student, we'll look for another A student.

Some financial advisors can't do that for their clients. They either don't have the technology or systems in place, or they simply don't have the time to do it themselves because they don't have enough employees to manage everything clients expect.

Many will open a brokerage account for a client and sprinkle in a lot of different things, but then leave it alone. They simply don't have the time or the infrastructure in their office to truly manage that portfolio. They may well have placed some very good investments there at the start, but if those assets take a turn and are not performing, they likely won't realize it until a disgruntled client tells them.

At Affinity, many of my clients have one of our investment models, or multiple models if they have multiple accounts and they want different levels of risk/return for each account. The risk/return level they are comfortable with may vary depending on whether an account is in their tax-deferred, tax-now or tax-favorable buckets.

By continually checking the performance of the investments in each model, and making changes when necessary, we work to help get the best possible return for every client in that model. This way we don't have to monitor each individual's account for performance, or prioritize one client over another. All get rebalanced at the same time. Most clients aren't even aware of the subtle changes. As long as they occur without fees or changes in risk level, we make these changes without calling every client.

Moreover, in the event of a drastic, major market downturn, we'll change a client's risk model into something more conservative without calling and saying, "Hey, do I have your permission to lower your risk in your account?"

If, however, I think the conditions are right for you to take a little more risk — to go from a No. 3 to 4, or 4 to 5 — I will call and discuss it. I want you to see what I see and ask if you agree it is time to take some more risk in the hope of getting more return. As conditions change in a client's life, or in the economy as a whole, we'll explore together whether it's time to change their overall risk tolerance.

It's also part of my job as a financial advisor to get clients into the right model, or models.

As an example: The accounts you want to be more aggressive are typically in a right-bucket Roth IRA. They are tax-favorable forever and do not have the age 70 ½ rules, so why not be a little more aggressive there? On the flip side, your most conservative accounts are typically in the middle bucket, the money you may need now. That's especially true when you're under age 59 ½. You want to keep some money liquid, and you don't want it fluctuating wildly if the stock market does. Your left-bucket, tax-deferred accounts can be middle risk, our middle model numbers.

Hope for the best, prepare for the worst

A key in money management is to always be thinking ahead to the next market downturn.

I use two different terms to describe the ways a market goes down. There are hiccups, and there are corrections.

A hiccup typically happens two to four times a year and can last anywhere from two days to two months. A hiccup can be very minimal, or it can be as much as a 6 or 10 percent drop in the overall market. Hiccups are generally caused by reaction to current news or events. The term hiccup also implies that the market will bounce back up in a short period of time with only a minimal loss.

A correction is rarer, coming every three to seven years. That's a big window, and that's good because corrections are bigger, typically defined as a drop of 15 to 20 percent or more. The last two major corrections resulted in a 55 percent drop from the third quarter of 2007 through the first quarter of 2009,[13] and a 45 percent drop in a period from 2000 through 2002.[14] The average correction can last up to 10 to 14 months, and the last two lasted 18 months — in the dot-com collapse and the housing bubble burst.[15]

For us as financial advisors managing your money, the worst thing we can do is be trigger happy, trying to time the market on every little hiccup. If you try to do that, you end up selling low and buying high. You will likely realize that you got out of something too soon — thinking it was going to get worse — then want back in at a time when the market is going back up. That's a worst-case scenario. You never want to sell low and buy high.

Look at it this way. Would you buy an antique or some collectable item for $100, then turn around and sell it to someone for $75? Of course not. You would ideally buy that item on sale for $90, then sell it to someone else for $100. The stock market works the same way.

But a second-worst case is holding on and trying to ride out a storm. Because you're in this for the long term, you hold on to everything during a major market correction, even if that means needing four years to get back what you lost in one.

That is exactly what happened to many people in the Great Recession from October 2007 to March 2009 when they rode out a frightening 18 months of losing money.[16] Following the bottoming out, the market started to climb again and was still

---

[13] The Dow Jones Industrial Average peaked at 14,164 on Oct. 9, 2007, and "bottomed out" at 6,507 on March 9, 2009.

[14] The S&P 500 fell from a high of 1527 in March 2000 to a low of 776 in October 2002.

[15] NBCNews.com. "11 historic bear markets." http://www.nbcnews.com/id/37740147/ns/business-stocks_and_economy/t/historic-bear-markets/#.V31AkFUrJhE.

[16] Constantine Von Hoffman. CBS MoneyWatch. May 31, 2013. "Wealth of most Americans down 55 percent since recession." http://www.cbsnews.com/news/wealth-of-most-americans-down-55-since-recession/.

climbing at the writing of this book in the spring of 2015. For example, it took the average investor about four years to gain back what they lost in the previous 1 ½ years. Doing the math, that is a combined 5 ½-year process of losing and then trying to win back what you lost. Your rate of return for that 5 ½ years was zero percent. It's hard to achieve your retirement goals earning zero percent over five-year blocks of time.

Worse still, this result was very similar to the previous correction of 2001 and 2002. This is why many people in financial circles call the first decade of the 21st century "the lost decade." It was especially horrific to baby boomers, who were getting close to retirement when the Great Recession came knocking, not far off the wake of the dot-com downturn earlier in the decade. Talk about taking a major blow to your retirement savings at the worst possible time!

What I share with clients as we watch the hiccups — looking to see if they will turn into a full-fledged market correction — is that they will lose some money before I get them out of the stock market completely. But I also make it clear that, in the event of a long-lasting market downturn, I will steer them toward more conservative investments.

The trouble, of course, is that there is no crystal ball to tell anyone whether we're looking at a typical hiccup or the start of something more dramatic. No one has enough information to make that call until we're well into the downturn. Anyone who says he can identify the top of the market right before it starts to go down is fooling himself.

It sometimes takes several days or even weeks before anyone can determine if a sudden downturn is simply a brief reaction to something in the news, or is something much more significant. A decline in oil prices, Russia fighting with Ukraine, a new conflict in the Middle East, Hurricane Katrina, a possible rise in interest rates — any news event can briefly affect the market.

But events happening in the world around us also can signal the start of really bad things to come. You need to ask if there is an underlying economic or financial issue — something with some real driving power — that is fueling a significant directional trend. Is this just a blip, or is it the bursting of the dot-com bubble or the housing bubble — the major factors behind the recessions of 2001 and 2008?

If that's the case — if we believe we're looking at more than a hiccup — it's time to get you out before the little money you've lost turns into a lot of money lost. Let's get into some protection — bonds, cash, fixed annuities, anything to protect you from a major market downturn. The prudent financial advisor doesn't let clients just ride out the downturn, but gets them into areas of more safety somewhere along the way.

The stock market sometimes acts like a roller coaster. Yet, in a world of frequent and unpredictable market ups and downs, there are some who actually believe they can make a miraculous exit near the top of the ride before it starts its wild, scary plunge downward. Then, in this same fantasy scenario, they somehow believe they can get back on the ride near the bottom and take it up to the top again.

Seriously, are there any amusement park rides anywhere in the world that operate like that?

Being patient through the frequent hiccups is hard, and we often must hold our clients' hands during this process. Remember, a hiccup is a short-term blip, and normal market function will likely resume soon.

The hardest part comes in trying to decide whether a downturn is more than a hiccup, that it really is the beginning of the next major market correction. This is when many investors want out, but by now we are already on the downhill plunge of the ride — unless you had the inexplicable luck of a lottery mega-jackpot winner, or owned a crystal ball that told you to get out before the fall. But for the 99.999 percent of the rest of us, now is the time to decide whether to ride the plunge all the way to the bottom, knowing it will eventually start its slow rise back up, or cut our losses.

I maintain that the financial advisor who doesn't offer "flight to safety" options to a client during these times is either too scared to make a call, or too busy to deal with you and your account because they've moved on to the next client. Typically those advisors are commission driven. If you lose money, it doesn't change their compensation because they've already made the sale. But it sure changes my compensation as a performance-based advisor.

I can make money through commissions also, but most of our clients prefer that I do not take that method of compensation. They prefer my compensation be based on their account value. That means that as we grow their accounts, we also make more revenue. Conversely, if their account values shrink, so does my revenue. Believe me, it's hard to run a business with rising expenses like payroll and rent when you have decreasing revenue. I can't exactly go to my landlord or employees and ask for a break in the rent or payroll just because the market is down.

Moreover, it should not be that difficult to advise a client to take money off the table.

In late 2007, we had just seen the stock market hit all-time highs. Then it started to tip and go down amid news of the failure of mortgage-backed securities and the subsequent closing of several giant companies in the financial world. After a period of about six to eight weeks, there was finally enough data and information from various economists and analysts to determine that this was more than just a hiccup, more than just a reaction to current events. They told us there was some real fuel feeding this fire, and there would probably be more to come.

Again, did anyone have a crystal ball to know how bad it would get? Of course not. But there was finally enough data available to say, "Look, we've been losing some money. Let's get out now before this gets a whole lot worse."

That's the time when you have to consider other options. Maybe it's time to look at all bonds, or all cash, or cash and bonds — anything outside of the stock market side of things.

When the market takes that big a drop, we at Affinity Asset Management get our clients out. We don't have time to call all clients and ask for permission to protect their money. Because we have signed authority from our clients to make changes as necessary, we take steps to protect their money when conditions require us to do so without calling them.

On the other hand, in more normal market conditions where we are not in a big downturn, if we feel the market is looking promising for some time to come and we think certain clients are ready to take on some additional risk and return, we will call those clients and ask their permission to move them up in risk.

Besides, what's the worst that can happen if you advise a client to get out of the market for a while? We get out, watch as the market starts to recover, then get back in before it gets too high again. This doesn't mean we're trying to time every little hiccup that arises several times each year. What it does mean is that we will deal with major market corrections that come every so often.

To be sure, we will hold a client's hand and urge patience during the hiccups. But, when it becomes obvious that the market is going down longer than the typical hiccup, somewhere along the way we have to make the decision to help clients in ways beyond just holding their hands.

Be ready for the rally

Having made the decision to cut your losses during a major downturn, the next tough decision involves when to get back into the market that inevitably (as history repeatedly shows us) will begin another ascent.

Again, lacking the insight of a lottery winner or a fortune teller, no financial advisor can accurately pinpoint the bottom of the ride down, or predict the absolute best time to get back in. In a declining market, how do you know whether you're looking at a good buying opportunity or a poor investment? Remember, too, that even the wildest ride down has the occasional uphill bump. Is this just a short-term pop before a continuation of the fall? Or is it the start of a turnaround that will last for a while?

It is only after we have enough information to gauge the upward direction of the market that most people gain the confidence to buy back in. But gathering this macro-world information is something many investors do not have the time to do for themselves, meaning the guidance of a trusted financial advisor is invaluable here.

We apply the same standards we used in telling our clients it was time to get out. Somewhere near the bottom or just beyond it, there will come a time when enough economists and analysts determine that we've begun the healing process and it is a good time to get back in the market. Sometimes that process can take six to eight weeks from the time we hit rock bottom. Again, this is because no one has a crystal ball to tell them where that bottom is. But when the rebound starts to look sustained, then it's time to make the call that the worst is behind us and it's a good time to get back in the water.

Now, having heard all of that, ask yourself this question:

What did my financial advisor do for me before and during both major corrections of this century's first decade?

Here's the reality. They probably did little to nothing.

Many advisors sell good products, and even call you every so often for a review. But they often have little incentive or process to get their clients out of a market in a major downturn. And if they do try to do so, it usually involves one client at a time, meaning they have to decide who gets rescued first.

Here's another question to consider. If your advisor offered you no "flight to safety" options at any time during the most recent market correction of 2008, if he offered no ideas about how to stop the bleeding, are you still with that same advisor? If so, why?

No question, most investors lost money during the Great Recession. But did you lose more than you were comfortable losing because you decided to ride it out? Or, worse yet, because no one gave you other options? What makes you think anything will be different when the next correction comes around?

We recommend you consider some alternatives.

No. 1, always get a second opinion when it comes to your money. You wouldn't hesitate to get a second opinion on something as important as your health. Why would your money be any less important?

No. 2, have a talk with your current advisor and ask how he or his company selects the investments in your account. Then ask how they manage those investments. How is your account managed compared to all the other accounts they service? Ask what process they use to buy and sell the investments in your account.

Finally, ask about their process in the event of a major market correction. More exactly, how do they get the information upon which they offer advice in a downturn? Do they actively offer clients alternatives, or are they of the "hold the line" philosophy? What do they do with clients' accounts once they determine that a major correction is underway?

Managing money, you must remember, involves more than just the advisor-client relationship. That relationship is important, no doubt. But, as is the case in a long-standing marriage, communication is essential with equal give and take on both sides. A one-sided relationship is hardly the best approach.

So, feel free to question your current advisor, and if you are not satisfied with the answers, go get that second opinion. Please do not rely solely on your relationship with that one advisor. This is your money, and although someone you've known for years may care a great deal about you, no one will care more about your money than you do. Make sure you are getting the information and services you deserve.

CHAPTER 9

Never stop learning

W e ended the previous chapter talking about the two-
way communication necessary between a client and a
financial advisor. For that to happen most effectively,
the former needs to have a reasonably good idea about what the
latter is saying.

That's why we work to keep our Affinity Asset Management
clients as well informed as we can about the things that affect their
money, and consequently their lives. Again, setting us apart from
other advisors, we do a lot of additional things for our clients that
other advisors just don't offer. Through periodic individual
reviews, group information sessions and semi-weekly blogs or
postings on our Affinity website, we strive to give our clients the
information they need to be an active partner in making the
decisions that affect them.

I often make it a point during a client review session to ask the
person I'm visiting, "Tell me, how are we doing here at Affinity?
What are we doing well? What are we not doing well?"

I usually get the same two answers. What clients love most
about our office is our people, which doesn't surprise me. I've
either been very brilliant or just plain lucky to have hired some
truly amazing people. My team cares about our clients' need for

information and provides attention to their transaction requests, and people understand and appreciate it.

The No. 2 answer involves our review process. People like being kept informed, which is an important aspect of what we do. It helps the client and, to be frank, it helps my company. Look at it this way: If all other things are equal — if my performance is the same or no better than another advisor's — why should I expect a prospective new client to consider me?

Well, the difference that may tip the scale could be the way we keep our clients informed.

We have a review process in which we call clients on a regular schedule several times a year and talk about how their accounts are doing. I don't know that many other advisors do as many individual client reviews as we do in a given year.

We talk about what's going on in the markets in addition to what is happening with their accounts and in their lives. These are individual, one-on-one reviews, mostly done over the phone, and they are quite productive. If people are traveling like many of our retired clients like to do, they aren't forced to come into our office. We make it easy for them.

In addition to those individual reviews we offer what we call our quarterly client education series.

We bring in financial industry speakers from major companies to talk about things going on in the economy or other issues of the day to keep our clients up to speed on the world around them. We've also done sessions on identity theft, estate planning and income tax law changes. Part of this may be similar to what they hear from me in our individual reviews, but there is usually additional material they are hearing from someone other than me, and clients seem to love it. They know there will be no selling, no product discussion, no commercial from the company the speaker represents.

We're active on the internet, as well.

Once every week, usually on Thursday, our own people create the Affinity Market Minute, which is about how long it takes to read. Our quick newsletter includes five to 10 bullet points, short and quick, about what's happening in the market, in the global or national economy, or in politics over the past week that might somehow impact the market and your investments. We also repost articles from major publications on subject matter relevant to the investment climate.

Knowledge helps develop trust

So many aspects of financial services, like in health care, come down to trust and relationships.

That's why it's important when considering a new relationship with a financial advisor to ask for referrals from his or her other clients. Since we cannot post testimonials, I will ask some existing clients — those of similar age and financial situation to a prospective client — if they wouldn't mind answering a few questions from someone considering doing business with us. Once I get their permission, I will connect them together.

When we do get referrals of people currently with other advisors, I try to be very sensitive to not tear down the things that person and his advisor have done.

Simply put, I don't believe I need to speak poorly of someone else to build myself up. We don't fire our family doctor just because we've seen a specialist. I approach new clients as if they are considering adding us to a team that includes their current advisor. I ask lots of questions and listen to what they have to say. If we come in and do only certain things for them while they maintain their relationship with the current advisor, fine. If we end up taking over completely, that's also fine. We understand we all have very different lives and very different distractions that pull our focus and attention away from our health and our money. So, we move in the direction and at the speed that each client is comfortable moving.

The University of Roth

Even as I try to be respectful of a prospective client's relationship with a current or previous advisor, I also will not hesitate to plant seeds of information, to tell people about things I think they may not know or have not been told by the current advisor.

For example, one topic we frequently run into is the subject of Roth IRA conversions.

Processing Roth conversions isn't rocket science. They've been around since 1997, and people have been doing conversions into them for a long time. Yet, many financial advisors don't bring them up very often for a reason most investors don't understand.

The reason? The advisor doesn't make any money doing them.

Now, if you went to a typical advisor with a 401(k) and ask to talk about rollover options, sure, they'll talk. Getting that money out of your company's 401(k) and into a personal IRA makes them money because they get paid to sell you an IRA. But they probably won't spend much, if any, time talking about moving that money into a Roth IRA, because that wouldn't make them any money. They'd be doing two things but only getting paid for one. I, too, don't get any compensation for talking about Roth IRAs with clients, yet I do it anyway at Affinity Asset Management.

I've done many speaking engagements with audiences of financial advisors only. They routinely tell me they don't have time to discuss Roth conversions or educate clients on why it can be advisable to pay a little tax today to save a lot on future taxes. Or, as I said in a previous chapter, most financial advisors lack the office staff or the time, as they need to move on to the next client.

This may be why many advisors don't talk much about moving money from the different buckets — specifically, making conversions from the tax-deferred left bucket to a Roth IRA in the right. It's just extra work for the advisor who's not getting paid anything extra to do it.

For example, many advisors may not point out that there were two different times since Roths came onto the scene in 1997 in which the IRS granted Americans the right to do a bigger conversion one year and spread those taxes out over multiple years. Exceptions were made in 1998, when the IRS granted a four-year spread of those taxes, and again in 2010 when a three-year spread was allowed. It is important for an advisor to know about these exceptions when it comes to making decisions about the timing of a Roth conversion.

I think this is one of the things that sets us apart at Affinity. We are willing to talk about the things you don't know, and I hope it's a reason people come to see us. Advisors all get paid in similar ways — to sell products, basically — but the value-added services, information and strategies we provide are things that not everyone takes the time to talk about.

In reality, some advisors are short sighted. What I mean is, if an advisor was thinking more about long-term benefits for a client, he would ultimately generate more long-term benefits for himself, as well.

To illustrate the point, we know that doing things like Roth conversions will generate some immediate income taxes for the client. But in the long run, we also know such conversions will eventually help a client save on taxes over time. These tax savings help the client's portfolio get bigger, and as a portfolio grows, so does the revenue for the fee-based advisor. Now, this may not matter as much to the commission-only advisor who got paid upon selling a financial product, but it certainly matters to fee-based advisors such as myself. For me to sacrifice a tiny bit of revenue today — such as doing Roth conversions for which I am not paid — in order to do something that ultimately benefits a client later is important for both them and me, and is worth the effort.

Turning investments into income

Here's another example of something reasonably simple that many investors don't know because they've never thought to ask.

An essential component of retirement planning is developing a regular, steady income stream from the savings and investments you've been making (we hope) during most of your working life. But how is that transfer done, exactly?

Well, the process itself is as simple as signing a form that links your investment account to your regular checking account. Each month, on whatever day you choose, we transfer a set amount of money from the investment account — money generated by the sale of investments in that account — directly into your checking account. Withholding tax can be taken out just as was the case with your regular paycheck.

Again, a simple process, yet people think there is much more involved. Once again, they don't know what they don't know until someone takes the time to tell them about the questions they should be asking.

The typical client — whether of high income or low, whether with an abundance of money saved or very little in savings — often doesn't know what questions to ask of their advisor. Moreover, many clients aren't always able to answer the questions we ask of them.

That's why I sometimes say I'm 60 percent financial advisor and 40 percent psychologist. A really good advisor shouldn't be afraid to ask difficult questions of a client. And if the client can't easily answer those questions, we must take the time to help them find answers. It's all part of unlocking their brain to help them better understand their current situation, and their future options.

CHAPTER 10

The culture of Affinity

In the 19 years I've run my own company, I've never been trained on how to hire or fire people. I've never been trained in the human resources side of the business, or how to handle the conflicts employees may occasionally have with each other. I knew I would have to learn those things along the way if this company were to grow.

That's why I say I've either been very lucky or very unconsciously skilled — probably a combination of both — to have put together our Affinity Asset Management team, of which I am extremely proud. Just since the start of writing this book, we have hired three more brilliant people to help us grow and, more importantly, to help me help more people.

It's a team I hope to expand as we look for more people to help more clients. Consequently, I wanted to close with a chapter describing our work culture at Affinity in the hope that prospective new clients and possible new advisors and employees might better understand what we are about.

I'm probably a quirky interviewer in that I don't know precisely what questions to ask of a prospective employee. I basically try to feel out candidates like I would a new client.

But there is one thing in which I'm a big believer. That is, there are a lot of things you can train a person to do, but you cannot train work ethic and you cannot train personality. That's why, in my office, I'd estimate that half the people I've hired have previous experience in the financial industry, but the other half did not prior to when I hired them. Yet they were people I wanted, and they've rarely let me down.

Let me share a story about how personality matters.

I was looking to hire a marketing director. A friend of mine referred me to a candidate, a woman I subsequently called and scheduled for an interview.

Three days before that interview, this friend and I were at a bowling alley, celebrating with the youth baseball team we coached. Suddenly he says to me, "Mark, look, there she is, the lady I referred for your marketing position." Turns out she also was there celebrating something with friends.

She didn't know who I was, so my friend took me over for an introduction. As we approached, she was just coming out of the food and beverage area with two pitchers of beer in her hands. Needless to say, she was a bit embarrassed at meeting me for the first time — just three days prior to a job interview — while double clutching two pitchers of beer. But she handled the situation masterfully, and with a personality I immediately wanted as a part of my team.

When we met again days later, I jokingly told her at the start of the interview, "I almost didn't recognize you without your two pitchers of beer." We both laughed, and we still laugh about it occasionally after her several years as my marketing director.

Projecting confidence is another aspect I look for in building my team.

I'm reminded of the first interview I had with a young woman who showed up in my office wearing a pink skirt, pink suit jacket, pink shoes (with really high heels) and a pink briefcase. If I remember right, I believe her resume was on perfumed paper and she even carried a pink pen.

Just picture Reese Witherspoon's Elle Woods character in "Legally Blond."

She was 22, maybe 23, not far removed from her college graduation, and yet she walked in with a kind of confidence that seemed to suggest she knew she had the office job she was seeking. She didn't have the experience of some other candidates, but her confidence and personality were infectious. Turns out that her work ethic was equally tremendous, and I consider myself lucky all these years later to have hired her.

Once a person joins our team, we work hard to cross-train our people so that, if someone is gone, we have someone else who can step in and do that job without our office skipping a beat. It's helped us put together a pretty good array of talent.

For instance, we have our own people in analytics who build most of our financial plans. We can custom build plans for each client based on their specific situation, then show them the difference between what their situation can look like when using tax strategies as opposed to not having tax strategies.

We also have our own people structuring our own money management models. We do all the investment research, place trades and back test our models for performance. It's our job to constantly research investments and prepare simulated models that eventually produce the right combination of investments to get the risk/return levels we're seeking on all seven money management models.

For our people without a financial services background — those who work in client relationships, business development, marketing, community relations or other aspects of our office — I offer the chance to help them develop their careers on the financial side of our business should they choose to do so.

Several employees without previous financial experience have studied for and taken the examinations necessary to sell insurance and securities. Not all who work for these licenses use them immediately in a selling role, but they do use that added knowledge to better serve our clients in matters of money management, building financial plans or generally serving their needs.

We also observe a four-day workweek here. Taking Fridays off in addition to the weekend days is an employee perk I think people appreciate. You can schedule doctor appointments and other weekday activities that require most people to take time off from work to accommodate.

I know I don't provide the perfect environment, nor am I the perfect employer. I know everyone would like to make more money, have more benefits and work fewer hours. We all want those things. But I think it would be hard for my employees to find a better combination of elements for both their personal lives and professional careers than what we have here. We've worked to build a great culture with great people and great camaraderie. I'm continually hearing our people say that I'd have to fire them before they would leave this place.

But enough of me talking about my company. For a different perspective, I've asked several members of my team to comment about how they view their experience at Affinity.

Tom Strandell,
Senior Partner

I used to have my own two-person operation, myself and an assistant, before I merged my company with Mark, who I'd known for years. Being part of a full-service company such as Affinity probably helps me attract clients I couldn't have gotten before.

People seem to appreciate having a bigger office staff available to meet their needs.

We work hard for our clients, but also interact well among ourselves and have some fun along the way. That perspective seems to be attractive to a lot of our clients who are approaching or are in retirement. They like the energy we have as a team.

Tie in that culture with the good job we do in managing money, tax strategies and financial strategies, and those are the things that set us apart and help build client loyalty. We don't have a lot of client turnover.

Kellie Banta,
Vice President of Operations/Marketing Director

A little bit about what makes us different at Affinity:

We provide educational workshops for our clients. We bring them in as a group and provide lunch, during which an outside speaker from the financial world presents insight and answers questions regarding the economy or current conditions in the financial markets that might affect our clients' investments. We also publish a weekly blog about current affairs in the financial world.

Something else I've found unique about working here is how Mark lets the team in on the hiring process. After he has identified a couple of candidates he feels are best for a position, as an office group we all participate in the final interview. We have our own series of questions regarding what works best for our team and how a candidate might fit in. We don't make the final decision, of course, but we get to weigh in with our thoughts.

Our culture is one in which we work hard and play hard. We have gone to Royals games, cookouts, birthday parties, holiday parties, Easter egg hunts and March Madness events; the point being, we enjoy working together and playing together.

Mark, in short, places a high priority on doing all he can for his staff, including providing continuing education for us, just as he does his clients. He will send us to any training we think will help us grow in our careers.

Missy Tullis,
Business Manager

I've been with Mark since even before he established Affinity, so I've been here from the beginning. It's always been like being part of a family where everyone has the interests of everyone else at heart. We look out for each other and do whatever we can to help out.

I've often kind of bragged to my friends about the great boss I have — very giving, very generous, someone who takes good care of his people. As an example: After working our four-day work week for several years now, I don't think I could go back to any other kind of schedule.

Mark also makes the point that, once a person has been here awhile and has proven themselves, he's willing to let you try whatever you think you're capable of doing. He feels it's your right to move up in the company, and that growth opportunity is something we appreciate. I now have my life and health insurance licenses, and Mark provided financial help to do that. He does the same thing for other people in our office who are trying to move up in this industry.

Mark Roberts,
Owner/President Affinity Asset Management

Back to me one last time.

To work at Affinity Asset Management — whether in sales, service, administration or analytics — you have to be a team player. We want our team to be as precise as a surgeon at their craft, but also be something of a general practitioner when it comes to knowing the duties of co-workers so they can fill in whenever help is needed.

Admittedly, I can be a micromanager when it comes to what I do for my clients in taking them through the financial planning process and servicing their needs. But I am not a micromanager of my team. I expect them to do their jobs without me hovering over them. My philosophy is that I want to spend all my energy taking care of our clients, and my team needs to take care of me so that I can do that.

As I said at the beginning of this chapter, I have never been trained to be a business owner, yet over time I have become one. I take great pride in having developed an independent, full-service financial company that offers services not all financial advisors can provide. It doesn't take long before a new client sees what we have to offer — good historic performance, good service and good relationships.

This isn't a knock on their current advisor. Rather, it is an understanding that, for them to have us help them achieve their hopes and dreams in retirement, most of the time there is more they can do — and need to do — than they are currently doing.

There is so much going on behind the curtain at Oz that people don't know about — often until they meet us. We don't profess to be smarter than anyone else. But we will do our best to give clients what they ask for, as well as tell them about things they don't yet know to ask for.

I've always said that one of the biggest fears people have is that they don't know what they don't know. Education is the key. We don't need to force clients into anything that makes them uncomfortable. We simply need to educate them about where they are, where they are going and alternate ways to get there. We need to expose them to alternative ways of thinking using the laws, investment products and strategies that help them more easily achieve their goals with fewer bumps along the way.

REFERENCES

[1] All references to tax buckets and the rules governing them are based on tax law in effect at the writing of this book in 2015.

[2] An explanation of mutual funds, their classes, and associated fees is available at http://www.finra.org/industry/breakpoints-disclosure-statement.

[3] An explanation of mutual funds, their classes, and associated fees is available at http://www.finra.org/industry/breakpoints-disclosure-statement.

[4] All references to tax buckets and the rules governing them are based on tax law in effect at the writing of this book in 2015.

[5] All references to tax buckets and the rules governing them are based on tax law in effect at the writing of this book in 2015.

[6] IRS rules and formulas for calculating RMDs can be found at http://1.usa.gov/1wdopmC.

[7] Larry Copeland. USA Today. Oct. 9, 2014. "Life expectancy in the USA hits a record high." http://www.usatoday.com /story/news/nation/2014/10/08/us-life-expectancy-hits-record-high/16874039/.

[8] To be fair and balanced; married and single tax filers results may vary based your standard and/or itemized deductions. Some individuals don't pay state income taxes and everyone's situation may be different. Results are based on your own tax situation for that particular year.

[9] All references to tax buckets and the rules governing them are based on tax law in effect at the writing of this book in 2015.

[10] "Back testing" refers to a process in which we use computer software (a Morningstar program at our company) to input a mix of investments to see how that mix would have performed

in a historical context.. We can test the rate of return, alphas, betas, standard deviation and fees.

Obviously, we don't have a crystal ball, so we don't know where the market is going. Back testing allows us to see how a group of investments worked together. Not all investments will grow equally. Some will grow, some will be flat, some will lose. When put together using various market sectors and industries as well as the right combination of U.S. stocks and international stocks, along with a stocks vs. bonds blend, we can see with back testing how this combination would have performed. Back testing gives us a baseline on which to create our seven investment models.

[11] To be clear, we advocate tax minimization strategies, but we do not give specific tax advice at Affinity Asset Management.

[12] "Back testing" refers to a process in which we use computer software (a Morningstar program at our company) to input a mix of investments to see how that mix would have performed in a historical context. We can test the rate of return, alphas, betas, standard deviation and fees.

Obviously, we don't have a crystal ball, so we don't know where the market is going. Back testing allows us to see how a group of investments worked together. Not all investments will grow equally. Some will grow, some will be flat, some will lose. When put together using various market sectors and industries as well as the right combination of U.S. stocks and international stocks, along with a stocks vs. bonds blend, we can see with back testing how this combination would have performed. Back testing gives us a baseline on which to create our seven investment models.

[13] The Dow Jones Industrial Average peaked at 14,164 on Oct. 9, 2007, and "bottomed out" at 6,507 on March 9, 2009.

[14] The S&P 500 fell from a high of 1527 in March 2000 to a low of 776 in October 2002.

[15] NBCNews.com. "11 historic bear markets." http://www.nbcnews.com/id/37740147/ns/business-stocks_and_economy/t/historic-bear-markets/#.V31AkFUrJhE.

[16] Constantine Von Hoffman. CBS MoneyWatch. May 31, 2013. "Wealth of most Americans down 55 percent since recession." http://www.cbsnews.com/news/wealth-of-most-americans-down-55-since-recession/.

ACKNOWLEDGEMENTS

At the time of writing this book in June 2016, I have been a financial advisor for 19 years. I have wanted to write a book for 12 years now. So why did it take me so long?

Well, a life that includes coaching three kids in what feels like a full-time, seven-day-a-week job, as well as dealing with a fast-growing company, has its way of slowing me down. Family is always my first priority. Though I wanted to write this book for a long time, I could not do so at the expense of my family, or by using time away from my clients and the company that I also love.

How did I find the time now? Well, it's been super hard to make some adjustments, but it helps when my coaching days are in a seasonal downtime, and my amazing office team has works seamlessly to the point that I can be out of the office and nothing skips a beat.

Everything on my calendar these days is prepped in advance for me. All client reviews are being done. All client calls into the office for questions or service work are being addressed. Between advances in technology and the brilliant and amazing people in my office, I almost feel like I can be outsourced. OK, not really, because I truly love feeling needed, and I know my people need me as much as I need them.

I know there are a lot of really good financial advisors out there with all the best intentions. But I think that what makes me a bit unique is the willingness to think like a business owner as well as a financial advisor. By that, I mean I know I have to spend money to make money, which means I have to invest in surrounding myself with talented people who can do their jobs and help our clients as well as I can.

With their help, I finally found the time to work on this book, a dream of mine for the past dozen years. The idea behind this book comes from years and years of new clients coming to me, or coming to us, saying the same thing over and over. "Mark, if this is that easy, then why wouldn't my advisor ever tell me about these things?" Or, "Mark, oh my gosh, I wish I would have met you five years ago, or even 10 years ago, and started doing some of these things."

Why would anyone be interested in what I have to say? A good question, and the answer provides the foundation of this book. People crave information and they want unbiased and honest advice and opinions on what they can do with their money. We all have three major priorities in common: our families, our health and our money. The final third of that equation is something I can speak to. This book is filled with years of experience that I am excited to share.

I couldn't do any of this, of course, without a foundation rooted at home that starts with my wife Amy, my best friend, my high school sweetheart and my partner for the past 21 years.

Amy knows I am a high-maintenance person. I don't have a problem admitting this. I like to play golf on Friday afternoons. I like to get up early and get into the office. I like to be at all my kid's events, whether as a coach or spectator. I like family time to be family time. I don't especially like grocery shopping, doing laundry or paying bills, and Amy seems all right with that. I'm the family's income earner, but she has the much harder 24/7, 365-day-a-year job. I simply could not do what I do for my company, my employees, my clients and our kids if it wasn't for her. Thank you, Aim, for all you do for me and our family. I love you.

I want to also take a minute and recognize my "core three" of Affinity Asset Management. This refers to my team of Kellie Banta, vice president; Missy Tullis, business manager; and Jaime Wigginton, operations manager.

If I have done one thing right in developing my company, it is being blessed, fortunate or just lucky to hire amazing people. I am a believer that, as an employer, there are many things we can train people to do, but you cannot train work ethic or personality. Everything starts there, and these three have allowed me and our company to grow. Surrounding myself with such great people allows me more time to help more people.

Jaime probably has the craziest job, which is making sure all paperwork is in good order and that all client monies are flowing from point A to point B as the client needs. That is a huge responsibility. She also has to coordinate the rest of the office so we know where client accounts are at all times. This is probably the most tedious job we have in the office and the easiest to make mistakes. But this girl is almost flawless.

The biggest contributor to this book I want to thank is Kellie. She is the one who kept me on track for all the various book deadlines. She is the brains behind almost all logistics of this book. Besides serving as company vice president, she is also our marketing director and just overall boss when I am unavailable. A lot of our growth has come in the time she has been with me and can be credited in great part to her. She may not realize this or ever admit it, but she has contributed to so many things that add up to an amazing, productive work environment. She makes far more decisions a day than I do. I love that. It is a great feeling to know she has my back.

Then there is Missy, who has been with me through so much change and growth. She has been with me for almost 10 years now, and I am sure she is as proud of the growth of our company as I am. She helps control almost my entire life, from my work calendar to my personal calendar. I often joke about her "job description" because there is no short description for all she does. Besides being intelligent, our resident techie and a super hard worker, this girl never has a bad day. Seriously, I have seen her upset only once in almost 10 years. Missy is the glue that keeps me together, who keeps me busy and keeps a whole lot of things coordinated and under control. We have a very serious industry and small mistakes are huge to clients. Missy keeps me and our office organized and moving into the future.

I want to say thank you to everyone at Affinity Asset Management, and I want to say "I love you" especially to my core three. Without all of you we would not be able to help all the people we help, and more importantly we would not be able to provide deeper services to those clients, services they just don't get other places.

– Mark Roberts, June 2016